OECD Urban Studies

Decarbonising Buildings in Cities and Regions

This document, as well as any data and map included herein, are without prejudice to the status of or sovereignty over any territory, to the delimitation of international frontiers and boundaries and to the name of any territory, city or area.

The statistical data for Israel are supplied by and under the responsibility of the relevant Israeli authorities. The use of such data by the OECD is without prejudice to the status of the Golan Heights, East Jerusalem and Israeli settlements in the West Bank under the terms of international law.

Note by Turkey

The information in this document with reference to "Cyprus" relates to the southern part of the Island. There is no single authority representing both Turkish and Greek Cypriot people on the Island. Turkey recognises the Turkish Republic of Northern Cyprus (TRNC). Until a lasting and equitable solution is found within the context of the United Nations, Turkey shall preserve its position concerning the "Cyprus issue".

Note by all the European Union Member States of the OECD and the European Union

The Republic of Cyprus is recognised by all members of the United Nations with the exception of Turkey. The information in this document relates to the area under the effective control of the Government of the Republic of Cyprus.

Please cite this publication as:
OECD (2022), *Decarbonising Buildings in Cities and Regions*, OECD Urban Studies, OECD Publishing, Paris, https://doi.org/10.1787/a48ce566-en.

ISBN 978-92-64-63968-3 (print)
ISBN 978-92-64-42932-1 (pdf)
ISBN 978-92-64-80129-5 (HTML)
ISBN 978-92-64-89357-3 (epub)

OECD Urban Studies
ISSN 2707-3432 (print)
ISSN 2707-3440 (online)

Revised version, June 2022
Details of revisions available at: https://www.oecd.org/about/publishing/Corrigendum_Decarbonising-Buildings-in-Cities-and-Regions.pdf

Photo credits: Cover © Gettyimages/DrAfter123

Corrigenda to publications may be found on line at: www.oecd.org/about/publishing/corrigenda.htm.
© OECD 2022

The use of this work, whether digital or print, is governed by the Terms and Conditions to be found at https://www.oecd.org/termsandconditions.

Preface

The COVID-19 pandemic and global megatrends, including climate change, digitalisation, the new geography of work and demographic trends, provide momentum to scale up efforts to reuse, repurpose and decarbonise buildings in many OECD and partner countries. Many recovery packages offer dedicated funding from different levels of government, and specific incentives to drive that transition as part of national governments' commitments towards a net-zero economy. The European Commission's Renovation Wave, for example, aims to double annual energy renovation rates by 2030, with the objective of renovating 35 million building units and creating 160 000 jobs by then.

Buildings and construction are central to the low-carbon transition, since they account for about 40% of global energy-related CO_2 emissions. The decarbonisation of existing building stock, where the greatest challenge lies, is a key priority in many OECD countries, given the low rate of new construction. In addition to reducing carbon emissions, decarbonising buildings also offers such co-benefits as better health, energy affordability and green jobs.

Cities and regions already play an important role in decarbonising buildings, thanks to their prerogatives and investment capacities. Not only do they own an important share of public buildings, but they are also responsible for land use and building code enforcement, and they are familiar with the local building stock and in close contact with citizens and local businesses.

Drawing on the findings of a global online survey conducted between July and October 2021 in co-operation with the European Committee of the Regions (CoR), this report demonstrates the potential of cities and regions for advancing the decarbonisation of buildings. It identifies key challenges and provides policy recommendations for both national and subnational governments. In particular, the survey showed that most cities and regions have developed their own plans and ambitious policies for building energy codes and public buildings. At the same time, cities and regions face major capacity and funding gaps that limit their capacity to ramp up such efforts. Collaboration across levels of government is urgently required to overcome these obstacles. The Checklist for Public Action provided in this report outlines key actions for national governments to establish the enabling environment, and for local and regional governments to unleash their potential to decarbonise buildings.

This report calls for an effective multilevel governance approach to decarbonising buildings in cities and regions. We look forward to active and widespread use of its findings and recommendations at all levels, and stand ready to support further action to develop and implement better building policies for better lives.

Lamia Kamal-Chaoui

Director, Centre for Entrepreneurship, SMEs, Regions and Cities

Organisation for Economic Co-operation and Development

Hirohisa Awano

Director-General, Housing Bureau

Ministry of Land, Infrastructure, Transport and Tourism, Japan

Foreword

The COVID-19 pandemic prompted cities to rethink how they provide services, how they design their space and how they can restart economic growth. In exploring paradigm shifts towards a "new normal", cities have recognised the urgent need to accelerate the transition to a zero-carbon economy. Many cities' recovery plans include steps towards realising a greener future, for example through measures to promote clean mobility, nature-based solutions or the circular economy, capitalising on increasing levels of environmental awareness among urban dwellers.

Buildings and construction are an indispensable component of such a transition, as they account for nearly 40% of global energy-related CO_2 emissions – and up to as much as 70% in large cities like Paris, New York or Tokyo. However, the rate of progress in decarbonising buildings is far below what is required to meet the goals set by the Paris Climate Agreement and the national commitments to achieve net-zero carbon by 2050. This is due to a variety of barriers, including high upfront costs; lack of consumer awareness; and the lengthy process of negotiations with renters, co-owners and a wide array of service providers. Urgent action that cuts across sectors and levels of government is needed to overcome these barriers, to accelerate and scale up decarbonising buildings.

The OECD has long been working on buildings from an energy and environmental policy perspective, mainly at the national level. Such initiatives have included the World Energy Outlook, sectoral energy analyses, national environmental performance reviews and specific thematic work on buildings. As part of the OECD programme on *Decarbonising Buildings in Cities and Regions*, led by the Centre for Entrepreneurship, SMEs, Regions and Cities (CFE), this report is the first attempt to document the critical role of subnational governments in driving the decarbonisation of buildings in a shared responsibility with national governments. Key findings and recommendations call for countries, regions and cities to develop effective multilevel governance approaches to unlock the subnational potential for decarbonising buildings. Building on the Checklist for Public Action herein provided, the next outputs of the programme will continue to support the production of localised data and analysis, international policy dialogues and tailored case studies to guide better policies and decision-making for future-proof buildings in OECD and partner countries.

Acknowledgements

This publication was prepared by the OECD Centre for Entrepreneurship, SMEs, Regions and Cities (CFE), led by Lamia Kamal-Chaoui, Director, as part of the OECD programme on *Decarbonising Buildings in Cities and Regions* in the Programme of Work and Budget of the Regional Development Policy Committee (RDPC) and as a contribution to the OECD 2021-22 Horizontal Project on Housing. The programme was championed and supported financially by the Ministry of Land, Infrastructure, Transport and Tourism of Japan and the Ministry of the Interior and Kingdom Relations of the Netherlands.

The programme and underlying policy dialogues were managed by Atsuhito Oshima, Senior Policy Analyst, under the supervision of Aziza Akhmouch, Head of the Cities, Urban Policies and Sustainable Development Division, in the CFE. Baku Kawai conducted background research and contributed to the initial design of the programme. The report was drafted by Atsuhito Oshima, with input from Baku Kawai, Ji-Soo Yoon, Jonathan Crook and Keisuke Takamatsu from the OECD Secretariat, CFE. Special thanks are due to Tadashi Matsumoto in the CFE, for his extensive advice on the design and implementation of the programme.

The report builds on the results of the OECD Survey on Decarbonising Buildings in Cities and Regions, which was conducted in co-operation with the European Committee of the Regions (CoR) from July to October 2021. Special thanks are due to the 21 cities and regions (see Box 1.2) for their responses to the questionnaire and feedback throughout the project. The authors also thank CoR for its co-operation in conducting and disseminating the survey, in particular Alessandra Antonini (CoR) and Jean Tanti (CoR), as well as the European Covenant of Mayors and Energy Cities.

The report benefited from experts' insights at a policy seminar, *Unleashing the Potential of Public Policies for Building Decarbonisation*, held on 9-10 December 2021, and a webinar, *Decarbonising Buildings in Cities and Regions*, held on 14 December 2020. Special thanks are due to the Ministry of the Interior and Kingdom Relations of the Netherlands, which co-organised the policy seminar, in particular, to Ferdi Licher, Joram Snijders and Bente Vedder, as well as to the speakers, Paula Rey Garcia (European Commission), Sara De Pablos (Council of Europe Development Bank), Zachary May (Province of British Columbia, Canada), Jérôme Bilodeau, Katie Hicks and Jamie Hulan (Natural Resources Canada), Matti Kuittinen (Ministry of the Environment, Finland), Yves-Laurent Sapoval (Ministry of Ecological and Inclusive Transition – Ministry of Territorial Cohesion and Relations with Local Authorities, France), Eva Kasparek (Federal Ministry of the Interior, Building and Community, Germany), Takashi Imamura, Harunobu Murakami and Yoshihiro Murakami (Ministry of Land, Infrastructure, Transport and Tourism, Japan), Jurgen de Jong (Ministry of the Interior and Kingdom Relations, the Netherlands), and Michael Blanford and B. Aaron Weaver (U.S. Department of Housing and Urban Development).

Furthermore, thanks are extended to all the stakeholders who provided comments on the draft version of the report, in particular, Ksenia Petrichenko (International Energy Agency), Duncan Gibb (REN21), Yannick Trottier (City of Toronto) and delegates of the Working Party on Urban Policy, as well as to several OECD colleagues, including Boris Cournède, John Dulac, Sean Dougherty, Andrés Fuentes Hutfilter, Alexandre Banquet, Claire Hoffmann and Stephan Raes.

An earlier version of the report was discussed at the 30th session of the OECD Working Party on Urban Policy on 23 November 2021, under the reference [CFE/RDPC/URB(2021)22]. The final report was submitted for approval by written procedure to the Working Party on Urban Policy of the RDPC on 11 February 2022 under the reference [CFE/RDPC/URB(2021)22/REV1]. The publication process was led by Pilar Philip, and the final version of the report was edited and formatted by Victoria Elliott and Eleonore Morena.

Table of contents

Preface	3
Foreword	5
Acknowledgements	7
Abbreviations and acronyms	13
Executive summary	15

1 Setting the scene for decarbonising buildings — 19
- Buildings are central to the transition to a zero-carbon future — 20
- New construction alone cannot transform building stock — 21
- Decarbonising buildings requires subnational policy actions — 24
- Objectives of the report — 26
- References — 27

2 Why are cities and regions important for decarbonising buildings? — 31
- Carbon emissions and energy consumption vary across cities and regions — 32
- Buildings and construction follow local patterns — 33
- Cities and regions face different policy environments — 37
- Decarbonisation of buildings offers multiple benefits at the local level — 38
- References — 39

3 What are cities and regions doing to decarbonise buildings? — 43
- Leveraging regulatory tools and frameworks for building decarbonisation — 44
- Supporting financing and business models for energy renovation — 49
- Creating locally plans and strategies tailored to local needs — 51
- Engaging and training local actors — 53
- References — 56

4 Key barriers to unlock for scaling up local and regional action — 59
- Despite their potential, cities and regions face major gaps in governance — 60
- The impact of the COVID-19 crisis has been mixed on decarbonising buildings in cities and regions — 62
- References — 63

5 A Checklist for Public Action to scale up building decarbonisation — 65
- The key role of national governments in setting the enabling environment — 66
- A Checklist for Public Action to decarbonise buildings in cities and regions — 67
- National governments can provide a common framework across cities and regions — 69
- Subnational governments can help realise building decarbonisation in cities and regions — 72
- References — 76

Annex A. Questionnaire of OECD Survey on Decarbonising Buildings in Cities and Regions 79

FIGURES

Figure 1.1. Share of new annual housing construction in total housing stock 23
Figure 1.2. Breakdown of residential building by construction year 23
Figure 1.3. Thermal transmittance value of external wall by building age (W/m2K), 2017 24
Figure 2.1. Disparities in household energy consumption per capita, large regions (TL2), 2018 32
Figure 2.2. Carbon intensity in electricity production by region, 2017 33
Figure 2.3. Annual heating degree days in metropolitan areas in the Netherlands, 2018 34
Figure 2.4. Share of old building stock in the Netherlands by province 35
Figure 2.5. Share of multifamily housing and single-family housing in the Netherlands by province 35
Figure 2.6. Average energy consumption by type of dwelling in the Netherlands (per year) 36
Figure 2.7. Average new construction rate in the Netherlands by province (all buildings), 2012-20 36
Figure 2.8. Local specificities and unique contexts related to decarbonisation of buildings 38
Figure 2.9. Primary benefits of energy efficiency in buildings recognised by cities and regions 39
Figure 3.1. Primary targets for building energy codes applied in cities and regions 45
Figure 3.2. Percentage of cities and regions whose public buildings require greater energy efficiency than national levels 48
Figure 3.3. Financing tools used in cities and regions 50
Figure 3.4. Plans and strategies for energy efficiency in buildings 52
Figure 3.5. Key priorities of cities and regions on energy efficiency in buildings 53
Figure 3.6. Measures taken by cities and regions to decarbonise buildings 54
Figure 3.7. Stakeholder engagement (business and utilities sector) 55
Figure 3.8. Stakeholder engagement (non-profit sector) 55
Figure 4.1. Obstacles faced by cities and regions in decarbonising buildings 61
Figure 4.2. Data and information gaps related to building decarbonisation 62
Figure 4.3. Cities' and regions' perception of the impact of COVID-19 on decarbonisation of buildings 63
Figure 5.1. Share of cities and regions that receive enough support from national governments 67
Figure 5.2. Type of national government support cities and regions require 67
Figure 5.3. A Checklist for Public Action to Decarbonise Buildings in Cities and Regions 69

TABLES

Table 1.1. List of responding cities and regions 26

BOXES

Box 1.1. Zero-energy building 21
Box 1.2. OECD Survey on Decarbonising Buildings in Cities and Regions 26
Box 3.1. Net-zero energy-ready buildings through shared leadership: British Columbia, Canada 46
Box 3.2. Energiesprong programme: Net-zero energy housing through energy renovations 50

Follow OECD Publications on:

 http://twitter.com/OECD_Pubs

 http://www.facebook.com/OECDPublications

 http://www.linkedin.com/groups/OECD-Publications-4645871

 http://www.youtube.com/oecdilibrary

OECD Alerts http://www.oecd.org/oecddirect/

Abbreviations and acronyms

BPIE	Buildings Performance Institute Europe
CAD	Canadian dollar
CAP	Climate Action Plan
CEB	Council of Europe Development Bank
COP26	26th United Nations Climate Change Conference of the Parties
CoR	European Committee of the Regions
EC	European Commission
EISA	Energy Independence and Security Act
EPBD	Energy Performance of Buildings Directive (EU)
ESCO	Energy service companies
ESG	Environmental, Social and Governance
ETS	Emissions Trading System
EU	European Union
EUR	Euro
EV	Electric vehicle
GHG	Greenhouse gas
Gt	Gigatons
IoT	Internet of Things
NDC	Nationally Determined Contributions
NZEB	Net-zero energy building, nearly zero energy building or net-zero emissions building
OECD	Organisation for Economic Co-operation and Development
PM	Particulate matter
SBS	Sick Building Syndrome
SME	Small and medium-sized enterprise
USD	United States dollar
ZEB	Zero energy building or zero emissions building
ZEH	Zero energy house

Executive summary

Accounting for nearly 40% of global energy-related carbon dioxide (CO_2) emissions, and sometimes up to 70% in large cities, buildings are central to the low-carbon transition. Decarbonising buildings, especially older stock, through energy efficiency improvements and renewable energy use not only reduces carbon emissions, but also generates co-benefits in health, energy affordability and the labour market. Additionally, global megatrends and the search for a green recovery from COVID-19 provide impetus for stakeholders to take action.

Cities and regions have huge potential to decarbonise buildings and offer place-based responses to the transition to a net-zero economy. They own an important share of public buildings, and are responsible for building regulations. They are familiar with local building stock and close to citizens and local businesses. They are already taking steps to decarbonise buildings, often with more ambitious goals than their respective governments. However, they face considerable co-ordination, funding, capacity, awareness and regulatory challenges.

Drawing on the findings from a dedicated OECD Survey on Decarbonising Buildings in Cities and Regions and a two-year policy dialogue with government officials and key stakeholders, this report makes the case for scaling up the role and actions of cities and regions for decarbonising buildings, through innovative data, analysis and policy guidance directed to national and subnational governments.

Key findings

- **Key factors that affect the effectiveness of policies to decarbonise buildings differ across cities and regions**, as is the case for the carbon intensity of buildings, share of old building stock, rate of new construction and housing affordability. However, in all cases, decarbonising buildings helps to create jobs, enhance well-being and increase energy affordability at the local level.
- **Most cities and regions surveyed (86%) have their own plans or strategies, but many face challenges in implementing them**. Ministerial siloes and institutional fragmentation, combined with poor monitoring and evaluation frameworks, rank among the major obstacles in turning strategies into action, and driving effective and outcome-oriented investment.
- **Cities and regions also experience major funding and capacity gaps**. Inadequate government budgets and human resources hamper effective policy development and implementation on the local level. This results in a lack of incentives for property owners, who face high investment and transaction costs for energy efficiency retrofits. In addition, insufficient skills in the workforce and the lack of access to information and financing for small- and medium-sized enterprises (SMEs) also limit further action.
- **Cities and regions are undertaking ambitious policy measures at the subnational level, which can be scaled up**. Overall, 88% of the cities and regions surveyed demand higher energy efficiency standards than the national level in building energy codes, and 25% even call for a net-zero energy level. However, there is room to increase the enforcement of mandatory building energy codes and develop effective regulations for existing buildings beyond the 65% surveyed cities and regions currently applying building energy codes to existing buildings.

- **Collaboration across levels of government is fundamental for overcoming obstacles and making progress on the decarbonisation of buildings.** In fact, 74% of cities and regions reported that they need further support from national governments, for example to scale up pilot projects and raise awareness among the general public. National governments have a critical role to play in setting enabling policy environments for cities and regions, taking advantage of their legislative authority and access to the best available technical and financial resources within a country.

Key recommendations, based on the OECD Checklist for Public Action

- **National governments can set enabling policy environments by:**
  - **Developing common policy tools and framework across cities and regions**: National governments can set up the needed regulatory framework; strengthen incentives for energy efficiency and clean energy; and facilitate access to data and information to raise awareness.
  - **Enhancing multilevel co-ordination**: National governments can create a multilevel platform to align policies across levels of government; facilitate the design and implementation of subnational plans; and incorporate multilevel policy actions into national plans.
  - **Providing guidance and support to cities and regions**: National governments could consider giving financial support to pilot projects; supporting capacity building in local authorities as well as industries; and promoting new technologies for decarbonising buildings.
- **Cities and regions can plan a way forward by:**
  - **Creating a common vision for a broad array of stakeholders**: Cities and regions should engage diverse stakeholders around decarbonising buildings and develop a long-term common vision, with a comprehensive policy package for both public and private buildings.
  - **Devising effective regulatory frameworks for decarbonising buildings**: Cities and regions should strengthen the enforcement of mandatory building energy codes; provide a roadmap for stricter regulations; and test functional regulations for existing buildings.
  - **Introducing a monitoring and evaluation scheme for policy outcomes**: Cities and regions should assess the local policy environment for decarbonising buildings; and develop outcome-based indicators to track policy outcomes against subnational targets.
- **Cities and regions can lead by example, by:**
  - **Leveraging public buildings and procurement for further private investment**: Cities and regions should apply stricter energy efficiency standards to public buildings; and utilise public building projects for encouraging broader energy efficiency investment.
  - **Promoting pilot projects**: Cities and regions should launch pilot projects and leverage green finance to boost energy efficiency investment in buildings.
  - **Encouraging innovative business models**: Cities and regions should promote innovative business models that can make energy efficiency measures more convenient, reasonable and meaningful, by leveraging public and pilot projects and co-ordinating demands for renovation.
- **Cities and regions can engage all stakeholders by:**
  - **Raising awareness among citizens and local businesses**: Cities and regions should consider one-stop-shop advisory services, and formulate clear messages on the benefits of decarbonising buildings.

- **Providing technical and financial support to low-income households and SMEs**: Cities and regions should incentivise energy efficiency measures in low-income households and SMEs, by providing technical assistance and financial help.
- **Building capacity in subnational governments as well as local industries**: Cities and regions should encourage capacity building and facilitate skills development in the local workforce.

1 Setting the scene for decarbonising buildings

This chapter sets the scene and offers a rationale for decarbonising buildings in cities and regions, and the challenges and opportunities this process presents. Buildings and construction are a central element in the transition to a low-carbon future. They account for nearly 40% of global energy-related CO_2 emissions and have the potential to generate co-benefits in health, energy affordability and jobs. Decarbonisation of buildings calls for subnational policy actions beyond new construction, in particular renovating existing buildings and reducing life-cycle carbon emissions. This report draws on the findings of a dedicated survey of global cities and regions. It documents why cities and regions are important, demonstrates key roles they can play and actions they can undertake, identifies key obstacles and provides policy guidance for scaling up and accelerating the efforts to embark on this transformation.

Buildings are central to the transition to a zero-carbon future

The built environment is one of the major policy areas driving the net-zero transition. Buildings account for about 28% of total final global energy consumption and 30% of end-use sector (carbon dioxide) CO_2 emissions from the operational energy used to heat, cool and power them, including indirect emissions from the electricity and heating (IEA, 2021[1]). Including emissions from materials and construction accounts for nearly 40% of global energy-related carbon emissions (UNEP, 2021[2]). Global energy-related emissions from the building sector increased by 25% over the period from 2000-17, as a result of the expansion of the floor area of buildings, despite gradual improvements in energy intensity (IEA, 2019[3]). In 2020, CO_2 emissions from buildings fell temporarily by 10%, due to the pandemic, but further progress in the building sector is needed to meet the targets of the Paris Climate Agreement. It is estimated that by 2030, the average energy intensity per square metre of the global buildings sector must be cut by 30% from the level that prevailed in 2015 (UNEP/IEA, 2017[4]). In fact, between 2015 and 2020, energy intensity fell by 5.7% and emissions intensity by 17.2%. Additionally, renewable energy only accounts for 14.3% of total energy demand in buildings and has increased by only 3.8% percentage points since 2009. In the period from 2009 to 2019, the growth rate in heating (2.6%) was particularly slow (REN21, 2021[5]).

Meanwhile, global urbanisation trends continue to boost the demand for buildings. It is estimated that the construction sector will more than double by 2060, with its materials use reaching nearly 84 gigatons (Gt) (OECD, 2019[6]). Given that current Nationally Determined Contributions (NDCs) in the aggregate are not sufficient to put the world on a path to limiting global temperature increase to well below 2°C, exploring the role of building policies in reducing CO_2 emissions has become an important task worldwide. At the 26th United Nations Climate Change Conference of the Parties (COP26) in Glasgow in 2021, businesses and government networks announced 26 climate initiatives on the built environment, recognising the urgent need for bolder government action and deep cross-sectoral collaboration to reduce carbon emissions by half by 2030 (Global Alliance for Buildings and Construction, 2021[7]).

In addition to advancing the Paris Agreement, energy efficiency in buildings can generate multiple economic and social benefits in urban areas.

- The economic benefits include creating jobs, alleviating energy poverty and providing companies with strategic investment opportunities. Retrofitting buildings for energy efficiency can create jobs for low-skilled workers (OECD, 2013[8]). In addition, reducing energy bills by increasing energy efficiency in buildings can help tackle energy poverty, a pressing challenge in some OECD countries. Given the long lifespan of buildings, real estate companies that invest upfront in energy efficiency can become more competitive by cutting their energy expenditures and reducing future renovation costs. Participating in retrofitting projects offers a strategic opportunity for a wide array of businesses in their environmental, social and governance (ESG) investment portfolios.
- Major social benefits include improvements in housing and household health from reduced air pollution and adequate indoor temperatures. The residential sector accounts for 37% of global emissions of fine particulate matter ($PM_{2.5}$), particularly from heating with solid fuels, which can pose respiratory and cardiovascular risks for residents (OECD, 2021[9]). Indoor temperatures are critical for residents' health, since poorly managed indoor temperatures can lead to symptoms of sick building syndrome (SBS) (Jaakkola and Reinikainen, 2001[10]), Energy efficiency improvements in buildings can help remedy unhealthy living environments. Building retrofitting programmes for low-income populations can also improve the quality of housing (e.g. in heating water and insulation).

Energy efficient buildings have attracted interest in the context of the green deal and COVID-19 recovery.

- The European Commission (EC) launched a Renovation Wave initiative that aims to double annual rates of energy renovations in the next 10 years and create green jobs by supporting energy renovations with public funding (EC, 2020[11]). To meet the European Union (EU) target of a minimum 55% reduction in greenhouse gas emissions by 2030, from a baseline of 1990, the EC is proposing to revise the Energy Performance of Buildings Directive (EPBD). This includes a new definition of a "zero-emissions building", considering its life-cycle potential for global warming, minimum energy performance standards for existing buildings based on energy performance certificates (EPCs) and ending subsidies for fossil fuel boilers (European Union, 2022[12]).

- Many national recovery packages from OECD countries include energy efficiency renovations of buildings as their key components. France's EUR 100 billion recovery plan, launched in 2020, included EUR 6.7 billion in energy efficiency retrofits in homes and public buildings. Korea's Green New Deal of July 2020 promised to refurbish public rental housing and schools to make them zero-energy level.
- Cities and regions are also on the frontline on investing in buildings in their recovery efforts. In their recovery strategies from COVID-19, cities have prioritised energy efficiency retrofits. The Metropole of Lille in France, for example, announced a EUR 66 million recovery plan that includes investment in energy efficient renovation of 3 000 social housing units, more than 3 600 private homes and 600 student residences in the next three years. The aim is to promote both job creation in the construction sector and to advance the low-carbon transition (OECD, 2020[13]).

New construction alone cannot transform building stock

The major cause of the recent global rise in total energy use in buildings is attributed to the increase of the growth in floor area (an increase of approximately 65% from 2000 to 2017). This will accelerate given the rapid population growth and rising purchasing power of emerging economies, which are predicted to account for 85% of the global floor area growth by 2050 (IEA, 2019[3]). Once constructed, the environmental impact of energy consumption by buildings will continue, highlighting the pressing need for immediate public action to ameliorate energy intensity in new construction. One key policy lever is to extend the coverage of mandatory building energy codes. In 2021, only 54 countries had mandatory codes in place at the national level globally (IEA, 2021[14]) In developed countries, rapid action is required to apply net-zero-emission standards to new buildings, to avoid locking in inefficient building stock and costly future renovations. In the EU, the Energy Performance of Buildings Directive requires all new buildings to be nearly zero-energy buildings by 31 December 2020 (EC, 2019[15]) (Box 1.1). Whether this directive reduces carbon emissions will depend on how member countries transpose these requirements into national regulations.

Box 1.1. Zero-energy building

The energy balance of buildings and housing can be reduced to close to zero by reducing energy consumption and increasing the use of renewable energy. Examples can be found in several countries, but no international common definition has been agreed upon.

The EU defines "nearly zero-energy building" in Directive 2010/31/EU of the European Parliament and Council as "a building that has a very high energy performance", as determined in accordance with Annex I. The nearly zero or very low amount of energy required should be covered to a significant extent by energy from renewable sources, including energy from renewable sources produced on-site or nearby. Member states are required to ensure that 1) by 31 December 2020, all new buildings be nearly zero-energy buildings; and 2) that after 31 December 2018, new buildings occupied and owned by public authorities be nearly zero-energy. In December 2021, the EC proposed the revision of the Energy Performance of Buildings Directive, which includes a new definition of a "zero-emission building" as a

> building with very high energy performance, where the small amount of energy needed is fully met either by energy generated by the building itself or by locally generated renewable sources.
>
> The U.S. Department of Energy and the National Institute of Building Sciences define a zero-energy building (ZEB) as "an energy-efficient building where, on a source energy basis, the actual annual delivered energy is less than or equal to the on-site renewable exported energy" (National Institute of Building Sciences, 2015[16]). Together with industry partners, the US Department of Energy provides a series of guidelines on achieving zero-energy performance in various building types and climate zones. By providing a broad definition on ZEB metrics and boundaries, the federal government aims to incentivise subnational governments, as well as utilities or private entities, to adopt ZEB measures based on local needs and conditions (U.S. Department of Energy, n.d.[17]).
>
> In Japan, a zero-energy house (ZEH) is defined as a house designed to reduce its annual primary energy consumption to zero by 1) significant energy savings; 2) maintaining indoor air quality through improvement in thermal performance of the building envelope, 3) use of high-performance equipment, and 4) introducing renewable energy use. A ZEB is defined as a building that is designed to increase energy self-sufficiency as much as possible and to reduce annual primary energy consumption to zero. This is to be achieved by substantial energy savings; by maintaining indoor air quality through reduction of energy demands by advanced building design; by active use of natural energy by passive technologies and use of high-performance equipment; and by introducing the use of renewable energy. Japan's government aims to achieve the energy performance of ZEH and ZEB for houses and buildings built after 2030.
>
> In 2016, Vancouver (Canada) introduced the Zero-Emissions Building Plan (ZEB). Zero-Emission Buildings refers to buildings that are highly energy efficient and use only renewable energy. The city of Vancouver plans to transition to zero-emissions buildings in all new construction by 2030, To achieve this, the city provides tools including limits on emissions and energy use in new buildings (City of Vancouver, 2022[18]).
>
> Source: European Parliament and Council of the European Union (2010[19]), *Directive 2010/31/EU of the European Parliament and the Council of 19 May 2010 on the energy performance of buildings (recast)*, http://eurlex.europa.eu/LexUriS; U.S. Government (2010[20]), *Energy Independence and Security Act of 2007*, http://www.gpo.gov/fdsys/pkg/PLAW-110publ140/pdf/PLAW-110publ140.pdf; Committee on Following up ZEH Roadmap (2020[21]), *Report by the Committee on Following up ZEH Roadmap in 2019*, https://www.enecho.meti.go.jp/category/saving_and_new/saving/general/pdf/roadmap-fu_report2020.pdf (accessed on 9 February, 2022). Committee on Following up ZEB Roadmap (2018[22]), *Report by the Committee on Following up ZEB Roadmap*, https://www.enecho.meti.go.jp/category/saving_and_new/saving/enterprise/support/pdf/1805_followup_summary.pdf (accessed on 9 February, 2022); Government of Japan (n.d.[23]), *National Plan for Global Warming Countermeasures*, http://www.env.go.jp/earth/ondanka/keikaku/211022.html (accessed on 9 February 2022).

Developed economies have slow population growth, stable purchasing power and a low share of annual new construction in total building stocks (Figure 1.1). Strict regulations on new buildings, though, will have only a limited impact on the building stock as a whole. Older buildings in developed countries have much lower energy efficiency than newer ones. Public action will need to include more than "new" buildings.

Given the large number of their existing buildings, OECD countries face different challenges. In the EU, buildings built before 1945 still account for 23% of all building stock, and their average insulation level (of external walls) is only a fifth of that of buildings built after 2010 (Figures 1.2 and 1.3) (EC, n.d.[24]). In general, a higher level of insulation reduces heat loss from buildings and thus offers both a more comfortable living space and energy savings. To achieve the reduction in carbon emissions required under the Paris Agreement, the rate of building energy renovations must be increased considerably, from rates of 1-2% of existing stock today to more than 2%-3% per year in the coming decade (UNEP/IEA, 2017[4]). OECD countries can thus not achieve zero-carbon transition in buildings without enhancing energy efficiency renovations in their building stock.

Figure 1.1. Share of new annual housing construction in total housing stock

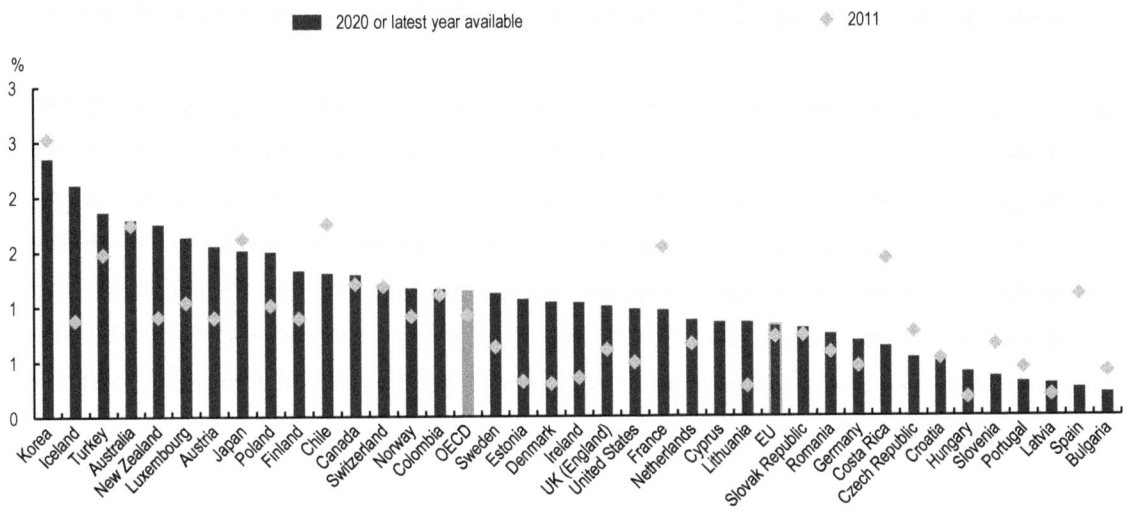

Source: OECD (2021[25]), *OECD Affordable Housing Database*, https://www.oecd.org/housing/data/affordable-housing-database/.

Figure 1.2. Breakdown of residential building by construction year

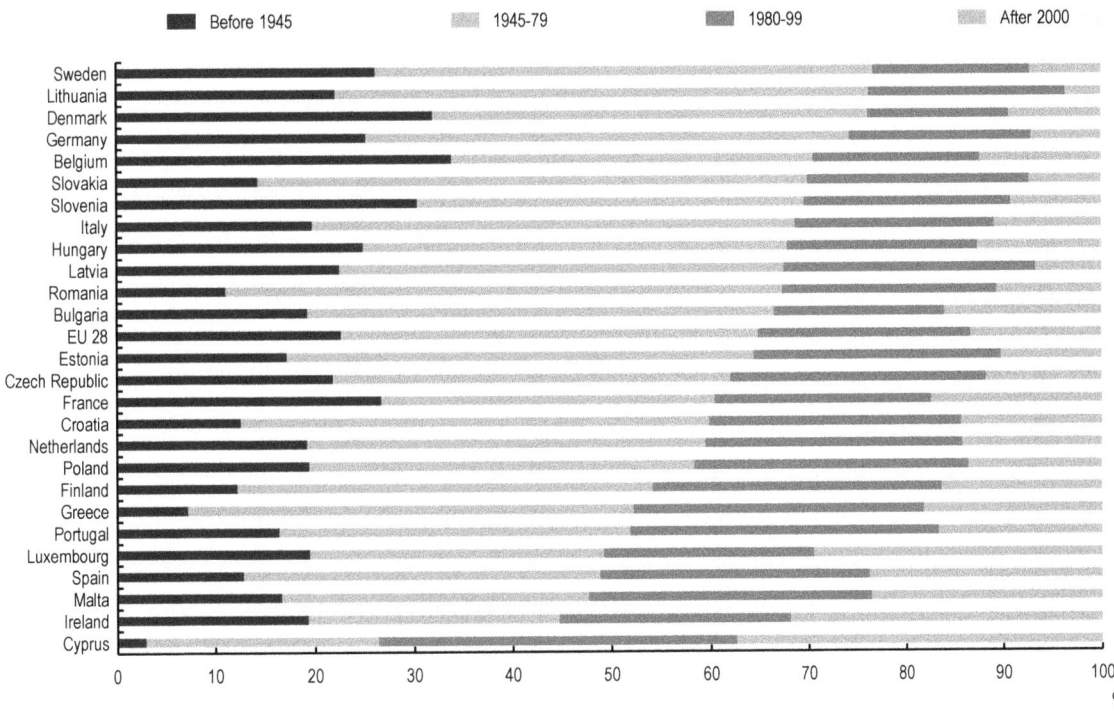

Source: EC (n.d.[24]), *EU Buildings Database*, https://ec.europa.eu/energy/eu-buildings-database_en.

Figure 1.3. Thermal transmittance value of external wall by building age (W/m2K), 2017

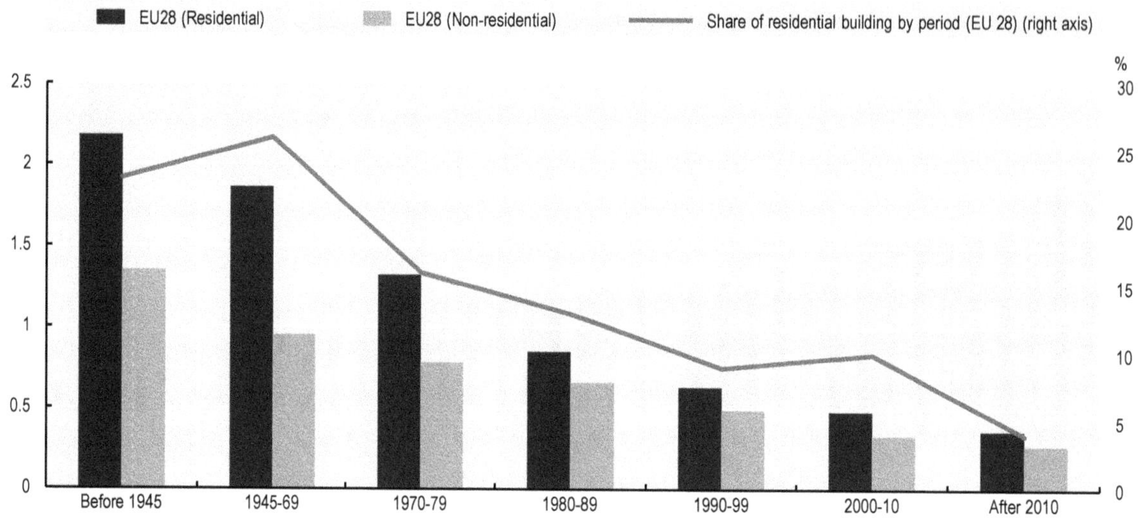

Source: EC (n.d.[24]), *EU Buildings Database*, https://ec.europa.eu/energy/eu-buildings-database_en.

In addition, energy consumption and carbon emissions need to be considered over the entire life cycle of a building, not only during the operational phase. The embodied carbon of buildings – all the CO_2 emitted in producing materials in the life cycle of buildings – includes all the emissions from the construction materials and building process and from deconstruction and disposing of the buildings (University College London, n.d.[26]). The embodied GHG emissions due to construction industries are approximately 5% to 10% of the entire energy consumption in developed countries and as much as 10% to 30% in developing countries (EBC, 2016[27]). These rates vary greatly depending on the country and region, but the carbon footprint of each phase of a building's life cycle should be taken into account. France has been one of the pioneers in pursuing ambitious policies to reduce embodied carbon of buildings. France's Environmental Regulation RE2020 requires the calculation of Life Cycle Assessment, which examines all materials and equipment used in a building from the construction and demolition phase. The regulation came into force in January 2022 (Ministère de la Transition Écologique, 2021[28]). In addition, incorporating circular economy approach will contribute to the decarbonisation of built environment through minimised material use and maximised reuse. Initiatives such as material passports, which provide digital data on materials used in buildings, or listing empty buildings, which could be used for promoting reuse and repurposing of buildings, can promote more efficient resource consumption and carbon emissions in buildings (OECD, 2020[29]).

Decarbonising buildings requires subnational policy actions

Decarbonising buildings means reducing energy consumption by upgrading insulation and installing high-performance equipment, as well as meeting energy demands with renewable sources as much as possible. Accelerating and scaling up the decarbonisation of buildings, involves a number of local policy considerations.

- First, buildings and construction vary across cities and regions, given that they have their own long histories of adapting to local meteorological conditions through local building materials and resources. Houses in colder regions typically have better insulated walls, while those in hotter regions traditionally include such features as longer eaves to reduce the heat gain. Urban areas have a large share of multifamily housing, while single-family, detached houses dominate housing stock in suburban and rural areas. The building stock of different cities and regions differs in age, size, tenure, usage and energy performance, and the strategies for tackling these buildings will necessarily differ. The rate of new construction and renovation is another important factor. Cities and regions will need to adopt different strategies depending on whether they have a large share of new construction. Urban areas, in particular metropolitan areas, provide greater opportunities for energy efficiency measures in new construction, given their population growth, while rural areas typically depend on refurbishing buildings to maintain their basic functions.

- Second, the policy environment also differs across cities and regions. Building owners include many private household owners, and policies to scale up building decarbonisation need to address housing and energy affordability. Housing affordability is an acute and pressing issue in large metropolitan areas, and the impact of decarbonisation policy on local housing prices and rents must also be considered. Housing quality is another consideration. The COVID-19 crisis has magnified the importance of inequalities in living conditions and access to housing in metropolitan areas. Low-income households were found to have higher risks of infection, due to poor housing conditions, lack of access to basic sanitation and limited living space, with three or more people in the same bedroom (UN Habitat, 2021[30]).

- Third, building decarbonisation needs neighbourhood- or larger-scale planning and co-ordination. For example, "zero energy buildings" or "net-zero energy buildings (NZEB)" have been gaining currency in many countries (Box 1.1). They need to be discussed at the neighbourhood or district level, because they involve district-scale energy infrastructure (e.g. a smart grid, energy storage, district heating), local renewable energy sources (e.g. solar panels) and innovative ecological building design (e.g. passive solar heating, natural lighting and ventilation). Developing mechanisms to finance building retrofits at the neighbourhood level is also needed in many countries. Cities and regions offer markets large enough to achieve economies of scale (e.g. mass production and financing mechanisms) as well as improvements in the quality of existing housing stock in many urban areas. Cities and regions can also take advantage of urban regeneration to accelerate the decarbonisation of their existing building stock. Decarbonisation of buildings also requires that construction and other relevant industries be prepared for the transition. Meanwhile, local authorities and institutions need to be conversant in code enforcement and certification of buildings.

Given the local nature of buildings and policy environments, countries cannot tap into the full potential for energy efficiency in buildings without subnational policy actions. Cities and regions have four major advantages in relation to the decarbonisation of buildings.

- First, cities and regions own public buildings themselves, and can use them as a catalyst for broader decarbonisation of buildings. They can promote exemplary pilot projects of low-carbon buildings, develop messages about their improved comfort and lower energy costs and pave the way for the private sector to invest in decarbonising buildings.

- Second, many cities and regions are responsible for building and zoning regulations. While building standards (energy efficiency, safety, etc.) are often regulated at the national level, local governments are responsible for local adjustment of the regulatory framework and for enforcement. Actions need to be taken throughout the entire building value chain to decarbonise the building sector. Local governments, especially cities, can develop ambitious regulations to promote decarbonisation, not only in new construction but also for existing buildings. In addition, local land use and zoning regulations determine what types of buildings can be built in which locations in urban areas. Cities are often better positioned than national governments to integrate these sectoral policies and generate synergies for achieving urban green growth (OECD, 2013[8]).

- Third, cities and regions are close to citizens and local businesses. Building decarbonisation requires a broad array of stakeholders, including from corporate property owners to individual households, and from local construction firms to energy advisers and local energy companies.

Cities and regions are in a good position to engage these stakeholders and coordinate to bundle dispersed renovation needs, including those of social housing, and to bring private investment into local renovation market.

- Fourth, cities and regions are familiar with the local building stock, whose characteristics and energy consumption vary greatly. They can take account of key local factors and develop tailored and strategic approaches to building stock. To unlock the potential for energy efficiency in buildings, a well-coordinated, whole-of-government and multilevel governance approach is urgently needed.

Objectives of the report

With this backdrop, this study aims to document the actual and potential roles of cities and regions in decarbonising new and existing buildings, and to discuss key issues and challenges towards an effective whole-of-government and multilevel governance approach that can contribute to the transition to a net-zero economy. More specifically, the study 1) documents why cities and regions are important for decarbonising buildings, 2) demonstrates key roles and actions of cities and regions, 3) identifies key obstacles that cities and regions are facing, and 4) provides policy guidance for upscaling and accelerating their efforts. This report is one of the first attempts to position the roles of cities and regions for decarbonising buildings in a global policy context and to discuss the importance of a whole-of-government and multilevel governance approach. The study is based principally on desk research (review of the literature, web-based public information), findings from a dedicated OECD Survey on Decarbonising Buildings in Cities and Regions carried out in co-operation with the European Committee of the Regions (Box 1.2), and the analysis of regional-level data provided by a specific case study on the Netherlands.

Box 1.2. OECD Survey on Decarbonising Buildings in Cities and Regions

To collect key data and information on the main trends, data and policies on energy efficiency in buildings in a range of cities and regions, and also on obstacles and good practices, the OECD conducted an online survey on Decarbonising Buildings in Cities and Regions, in co-operation with the European Committee of the Regions (CoR). The survey was conducted from mid-July to early October 2021 and primarily addressed authorities responsible for energy efficiency in buildings in municipalities and regional governments.

Table 1.1. List of responding cities and regions

Types of cities and regions	Cities and regions that responded
Regions (4)	Córdoba (Argentina), Emilia Romagna (Italy), North Holland (Netherlands), Tottori (Japan)
Intermediary entity (in countries with 3 levels of subnational government (1)	Scania (Sweden)
Municipalities (with more than 500 000 inhabitants) (8)	Rio de Janeiro (Brazil), Rotterdam (Netherlands), San Francisco (US), San Jose (US), Stockholm (Sweden), Toronto (Canada), Vienna (Austria), Yokohama (Japan)
Municipalities (of 200 000 to 500 000 inhabitants) (4)	Mannheim (Germany), Nilüfer (Turkey), Oakland (US), Tilburg (Netherlands)
Municipalities (of 50 000 to 200 000 inhabitants) (1)	Assen (Netherlands)
Municipalities (of under 50 000 inhabitants) (3)	Chorzele (Poland), Milanówek (Poland), Płońsk (Poland)

Source: OECD Survey on Decarbonising Buildings in Cities and Regions.

> The survey consisted of questions on subnational policies and challenges and data inquiries on indicators related to energy efficiency in buildings and related local factors (Annex A). In total, 21 cities and regions responded to the survey, including 4 regions, 1 intermediary entity (in countries with 3 levels of subnational government: department, province, county, etc.) and 16 municipalities of all sizes (8 of more than 500 000 inhabitants, 4 of 200 000 to 500 000 inhabitants, 1 of 50 000 to 200 000 inhabitants and 3 of under 50 000 inhabitants).

References

City of Vancouver (2022), *City of Vancouver*, https://vancouver.ca/green-vancouver/zero-emissions-buildings.aspx (accessed on 20 January 2022). [18]

Committee on Following Up ZEB Roadmap (2018), *Report by the Committee on Following up ZEB Roadmap*, https://www.enecho.meti.go.jp/category/saving_and_new/saving/enterprise/support/pdf/1805_followup_summary.pdf (accessed on 9 February, 2022). [22]

Committee on Following up ZEH Roadmap (2020), *Report by the Committee on Following Up ZEH Roadmap in 2019*, https://www.enecho.meti.go.jp/category/saving_and_new/saving/general/pdf/roadmap-fu_report2020.pdf (accessed on 9 February, 2022). [21]

EBC (2016), *Evaluation of Embodied Energy and CO2eq for Building Construction*, http://www.iea-ebc.org/Data/publications/EBC_Annex_57_Results_Overview.pdf (accessed on 29 January 2022). [27]

EC (2020), "Renovation wave: Doubling the renovation rate to cut emissions, boost recovery and reduce energy poverty", European Commission, https://ec.europa.eu/commission/presscorner/detail/en/ip_20_1835 (accessed on 15 November, 2021). [11]

EC (2019), *Energy Performance of Buildings Directive*, European Commission, https://ec.europa.eu/energy/topics/energy-efficiency/energy-efficient-buildings/energy-performance-buildings-directive_en (accessed on 30 November 2020). [15]

EC (n.d.), *EU Buildings Database*, European Commission, https://ec.europa.eu/energy/eu-buildings-database_en. [24]

European Parliament and Council of the European Union (2010), *Directive 2010/31/EU of the European Parliament and the Council of 19 May 2010 on the energy performance of buildings (recast)*, http://eurlex.europa.eu/LexUriS. [19]

European Union (2022), *Revision of the Energy Performance of Buildings Directive: Fit for 55 Package*, http://06 February, 2022. [12]

Global Alliance for Buildings and Construction (2021), "Accelerating deep collaboration: 26 built environment climate action initiatives announced at COP26", https://globalabc.org/index.php/media-global-advocacy/press-releases (accessed on 15 November, 2021). [7]

Government of Japan (n.d.), *National Plan for Global Warming Countermeasures*, http://www.env.go.jp/earth/ondanka/keikaku/211022.html (accessed on 9 February 2022). [23]

IEA (2021), *Energy Efficiency 2021*, https://iea.blob.core.windows.net/assets/9c30109f-38a7-4a0b-b159-47f00d65e5be/EnergyEfficiency2021.pdf (accessed on 10 January 2022). [14]

IEA (2021), *World Energy Outlook 2021*, https://www.iea.org/reports/world-energy-outlook-2021 (accessed on 29 January 2022). [1]

IEA (2019), *The Perspectives for the Clean Energy Transition: The Critical Role of Buildings*, http://www.iea.org/publications/reports/PerspectivesfortheCleanEnergyTransition/. [3]

Jaakkola, J. and L. Reinikainen (2001), "Effects of temperature and humidification in the office environment", *Archives of Environmental and Occupational Health*, Vol. 56/4, pp. 365-368. [10]

Ministère de la Transition Écologique (2021), *RE2020 Éco-construire pour le comfort de tous*, https://www.ecologie.gouv.fr/sites/default/files/2021.02.18_DP_RE2020_EcoConstruire_0.pdf (accessed on 29 January 2022). [28]

National Institute of Building Sciences (2015), *A Common Definition for Zero Energy Buildings*, https://www.energy.gov/sites/default/files/2015/09/f26/bto_common_definition_zero_energy_buildings_093015.pdf. [16]

OECD (2021), *OECD Affordable Housing Database*, OECD, Paris, https://www.oecd.org/housing/data/affordable-housing-database/. [25]

OECD (2021), *OECD Housing Policy Toolkit – Synthesis Report*, https://www.oecd.org/mcm/OECD%20Housing%20Policy%20Toolkit%20%E2%80%93%20Synthesis%20Report.pdf. [9]

OECD (2020), "Cities policy responses", *OECD Policy Responses to Coronavirus (COVID-19)*, OECD, Paris, https://www.oecd.org/coronavirus/policy-responses/cities-policy-responses-fd1053ff/ (accessed on 24 October, 2021). [13]

OECD (2020), *The Circular Economy in Cities and Regions: Synthesis Report*, OECD Urban Studies, OECD Publishing, Paris, https://doi.org/10.1787/10ac6ae4-en. [29]

OECD (2019), *Global Material Resources Outlook to 2060: Economic Drivers and Environmental Consequences*, OECD Publishing, Paris, https://dx.doi.org/10.1787/9789264307452-en. [6]

OECD (2013), *Green Growth in Cities*, OECD Green Growth Studies, OECD Publishing, Paris, https://dx.doi.org/10.1787/9789264195325-en. [8]

REN21 (2021), *Renewables 2021 Global Status Report*, https://www.ren21.net/wp-content/uploads/2019/05/GSR2021_Full_Report.pdf. [5]

U.S. Department of Energy (n.d.), *Zero Energy Buildings*, https://www.energy.gov/eere/buildings/zero-energy-buildings. [17]

U.S. Government (2010), *Energy Independence and Security Act of 2007*, http://www.gpo.gov/fdsys/pkg/PLAW-110publ140/pdf/PLAW-110publ140.pdf. [20]

UN Habitat (2021), *Cities and Pandemics: Towards a More Just, Green and Healthy Future*, https://unhabitat.org/sites/default/files/2021/03/cities_and_pandemics-towards_a_more_just_green_and_healthy_future_un-habitat_2021.pdf. [30]

UNEP (2021), *2021 Global Status Report for Buildings and Construction: Towards a Zero-emission, Efficient and Resilient Buildings and Construction Sector*, United Nations Environment Programme, https://globalabc.org/resources/publications/2021-global-status-report-buildings-and-construction (accessed on 26 October, 2021). [2]

UNEP/IEA (2017), *Global Status Report 2017 - Towards a Zero-emission, Efficient and Resilient Buildings and Construction Sector*, United Nations Environment Programme and International Energy Agency, https://globalabc.org/resources/publications/2017-global-status-report-buildings-and-construction (accessed on 30 November 2020). [4]

University College London (n.d.), *Refurbishment & Demolition of Housing Embodied Carbon: Factsheet*, https://www.ucl.ac.uk/engineering-exchange/sites/engineering-exchange/files/fact-sheet-embodied-carbon-social-housing.pdf (accessed on 29 January 2022). [26]

2 Why are cities and regions important for decarbonising buildings?

This chapter documents why cities and regions are important for the decarbonisation of buildings, and discusses the factors that influence local variations in policy and the multiple benefits generated at the local scale. Carbon emissions and energy consumption in buildings vary across cities and regions. In addition, buildings and construction are local in nature, with unique climatic conditions, varying building stock, and differences in the speed of new construction and renovation. Cities and regions face varying issues, including housing affordability, energy poverty and lack of capacity in government and local industries. The benefits of building decarbonisation at the local level include job creation, well-being and more affordable energy.

Carbon emissions and energy consumption vary across cities and regions

The share of carbon emissions from buildings varies across cities and regions. Buildings accounted for 28% of global energy-related emissions in 2018 (IEA, 2019[1]). In large cities, these percentages are even greater. Greenhouse gases (GHGs) or carbone dioxide (CO_2) emissions from buildings in London, Tokyo, Paris and New York were measured at 76%, 71%, 70% and 67% recently (Greater London Authority, 2018[2]; Tokyo Metropolitan Government Bureau of Environment, 2018[3]; City of Paris and Paris Climate Agency, 2020[4]; New York City Mayor's Office of Sustainability, 2017[5]). Comparing the share of greenhouse gas emissions from the building sector by type of region, the share is the highest in large metropolitan regions and the lowest in remote regions (OECD, 2021[6]).

Energy efficiency investments in buildings offer huge potential for reducing energy consumption and GHG emissions, but energy consumption per capita varies across the cities and regions in a country. Within OECD countries, household energy consumption per capita in the region with the highest consumption is typically three times higher than in the region with the lowest consumption (Figure 2.1). Different cities and regions diverge in outlook for energy consumption per capita. This can be partly attributed to the various modes they have adopted for water heating, space cooling and heating, or lighting, depending on unique geographical or climatic conditions, but also on different types of urban forms.

Figure 2.1. Disparities in household energy consumption per capita, large regions (TL2), 2018

% deviation from country average of electricity and heat consumed at home (kilogrammes of oil equivalent)

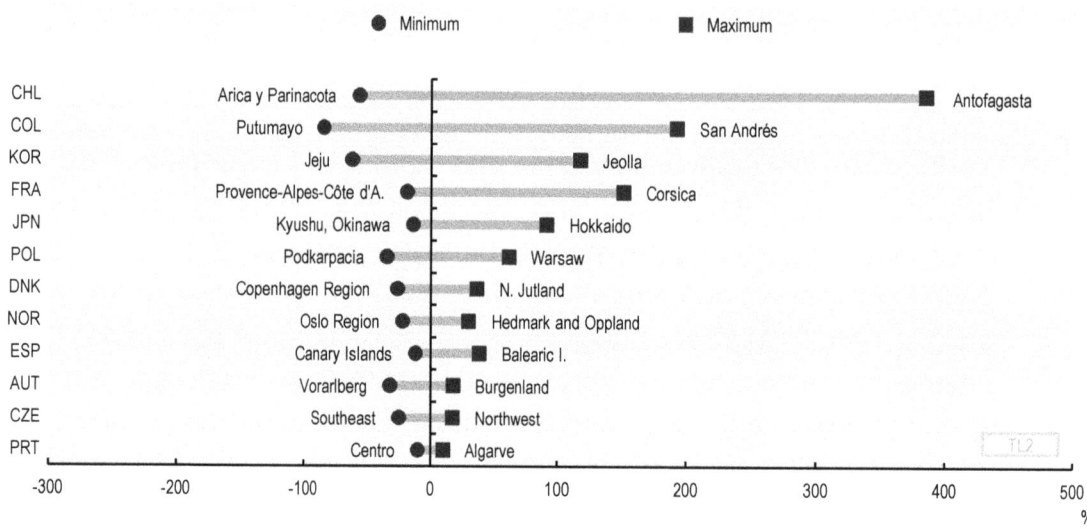

Note: Household energy consumption includes water heating, space cooling and heating, cooking, lighting and electrical appliances but excludes transport and consumption outside the house.
Source: OECD (2020[7]), *OECD Regions and Cities at a Glance 2020*, https://dx.doi.org/10.1787/959d5ba0-en.

The energy mix differs across countries as well as regions. Countries such as Sweden, Brazil or France, with a larger share of low-carbon energy sources (i.e. renewables and nuclear), have much lower per capita carbon emissions in general for the same per capita energy consumption (OECD, 2021[8]). Even within the same country, the carbon intensity of electricity varies across regions, and remote regions tend to have the lowest carbon intensity, with the highest share of electricity from renewable sources (Figure 2.2). Electricity accounts for a significant share of energy consumption in buildings (e.g. 25% of household energy consumption in the European Union (EU) (European Commission, 2021[9]) and 43% in the US (U.S. Energy Information Administration, 2021[10]). This regional diversity affects the capacity of realising net-zero-energy buildings at local scale, and by extension, local strategies for decarbonising buildings. At the same time, cold regions with low-carbon electricity often have high building emissions, due to fossil fuel heating. Subnational authorities may not be able to control the average carbon intensity of electricity, which is subject to change, given energy prices and national energy policies. However, they can support electrification and clean power by promoting energy efficiency in buildings and efficient electric equipment, like heat pumps.

Figure 2.2. Carbon intensity in electricity production by region, 2017

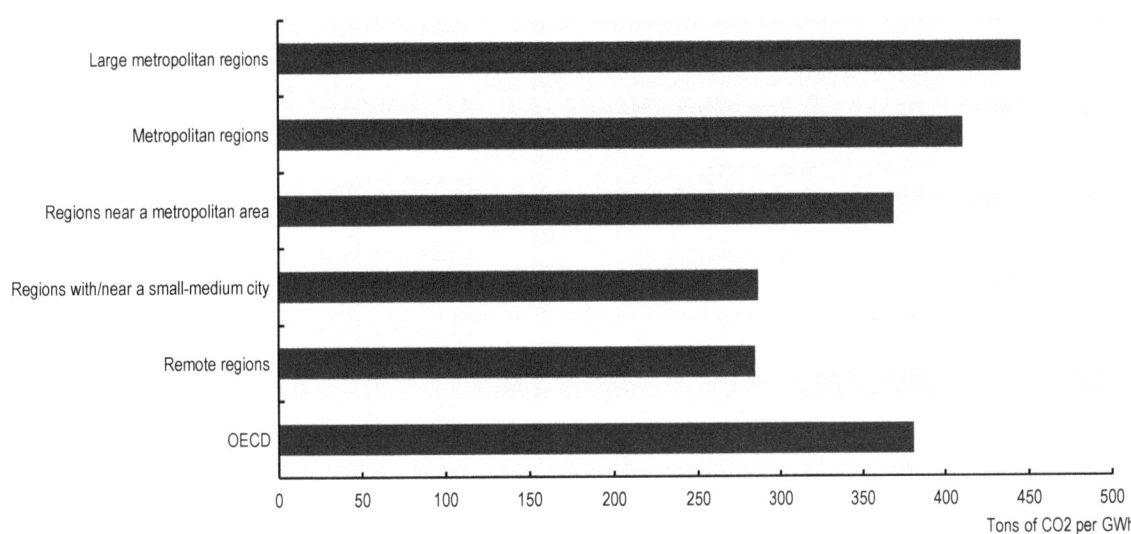

Source: OECD (2020[11]), "The role of regions and cities towards a climate-neutral economy (SDG 13)", https://dx.doi.org/10.1787/6acbc792-en.

Buildings and construction follow local patterns

While each country and region has a different energy mix, buildings within a given country also differ across regions, given the country's climatic conditions, the composition of the existing building stock and the speed of new construction and renovations. For example, a detailed spotlight of the situation in the Netherlands helps document such regional disparities, based on data provided by the Ministry of the Interior and Kingdom Relations.

Climatic conditions affect the energy performance of buildings that households and businesses require and also the property owners' motivation to invest in energy efficiency. Energy in buildings is consumed in the form of heat (e.g. cooking, heating) and electricity (e.g. TV, lights, air conditioning). The amount of energy used for heating and cooling varies greatly depending on geographic and climatic conditions, across and within countries. In general, households in colder regions consume larger amounts of energy for heating, which explains the larger per capita energy consumption in these regions, but also means that property owners have a strong financial incentive to make energy efficiency investments in heating. "Annual heating degree days" are one indicator that indicates a location's heating needs. The indicator represents the sum over a year of the differences between the threshold temperature (15.5°C) and the daily mean outdoor temperature, when the daily mean outdoor temperature is below 15.5°C. Figure 2.3 shows how heating degree days differ greatly within the Netherlands, from 1 716 in The Hague, to 2 175 in Groningen. The implication is that cities have different heating needs and adopt different strategies.

Figure 2.3. Annual heating degree days in metropolitan areas in the Netherlands, 2018

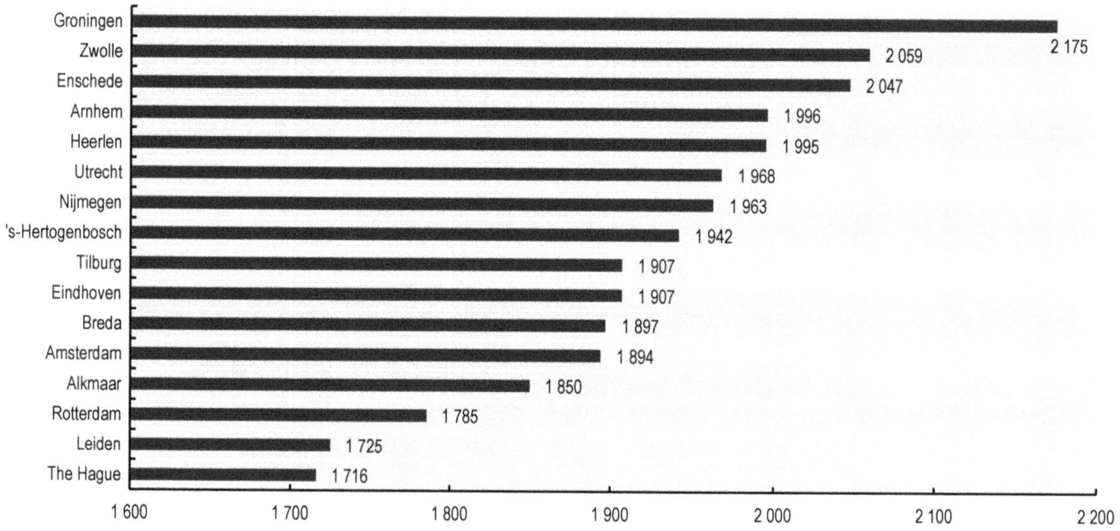

Metropolitan area	Heating degree days
Groningen	2 175
Zwolle	2 059
Enschede	2 047
Arnhem	1 996
Heerlen	1 995
Utrecht	1 968
Nijmegen	1 963
's-Hertogenbosch	1 942
Tilburg	1 907
Eindhoven	1 907
Breda	1 897
Amsterdam	1 894
Alkmaar	1 850
Rotterdam	1 785
Leiden	1 725
The Hague	1 716

Note: Annual heating degree days is the sum over a year of the differences between the threshold temperature (15.5°C) and the daily mean outdoor temperature, when the daily mean outdoor temperature is below 15.5°C.
Source: OECD (n.d.[12]), *OECD Metropolitan Database*, https://stats.oecd.org/Index.aspx?Datasetcode=CITIES.

In warmer regions, increasing use of air conditioners raises concerns and requires policy attention. It is estimated that without energy efficiency measures, energy demand in cooling will triple globally by 2050, and that space cooling will become the fastest-growing use of energy in buildings (IEA, 2018[13]). Due to climate change, even the coldest regions have seen an increase in average temperature in recent decades, which has increased demand for air-conditioning and other cooling systems.

Composition of existing building stock by age, by scale, by tenure or by use varies across regions. This influences buildings' energy performance, as well as potential targets for investment and barriers associated with building types. While data on the energy performance of the existing building stock is the key to identifying the worst-performing buildings, the age of buildings can be used as a proxy if such data are not available. Better data on the tenure of buildings could also help to guide the design and implementation of appropriate policy tools, since tenure status can present barriers to energy efficiency investments. In the case of buildings with multiple owners, the owners' individual vested interests may prevent them from reaching agreement on building renovation plans. Owners and renters may have "split incentives", because investment in energy efficiency may not necessarily benefit the parties that invest more. For instance, when owners invest in improving the energy efficiency of a building, it is typically the tenants who primarily profit from the energy savings (Erbach, 2015[14]).

The share of old building stock differs significantly across regions in the Netherlands. The percentage of buildings built before 1945 varies from close to zero in Flevoland, the most recently reclaimed province in the Netherlands, to 27.2% in Noord-Holland, where Amsterdam is located. The share of buildings built before 1980 also varies across regions, if not as much as housing built before 1945. Since older buildings generally consume much higher amounts of energy, the urgency and need for public policies and investment in decarbonising buildings also vary across regions (Figure 2.4).

Figure 2.4. Share of old building stock in the Netherlands by province

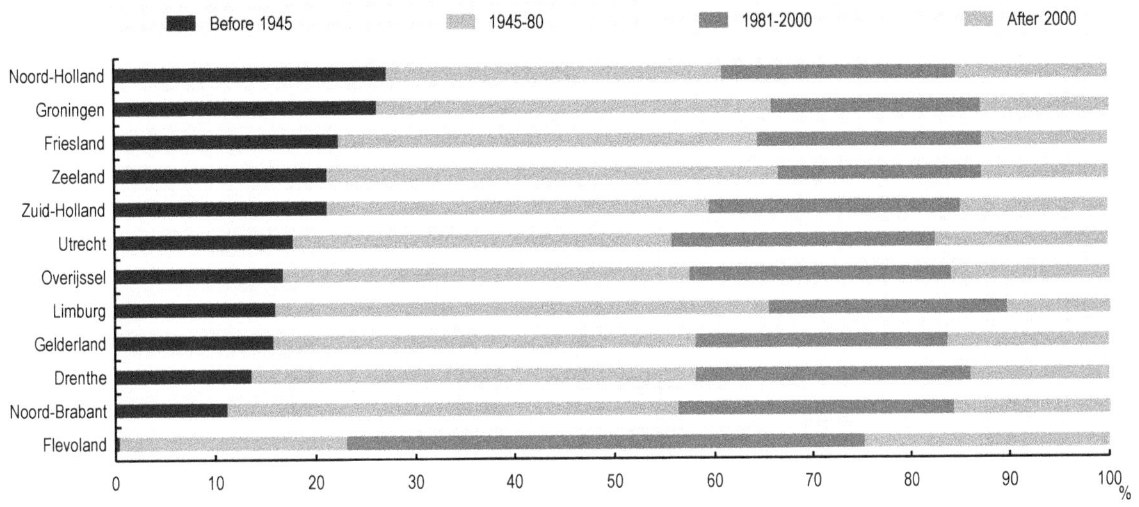

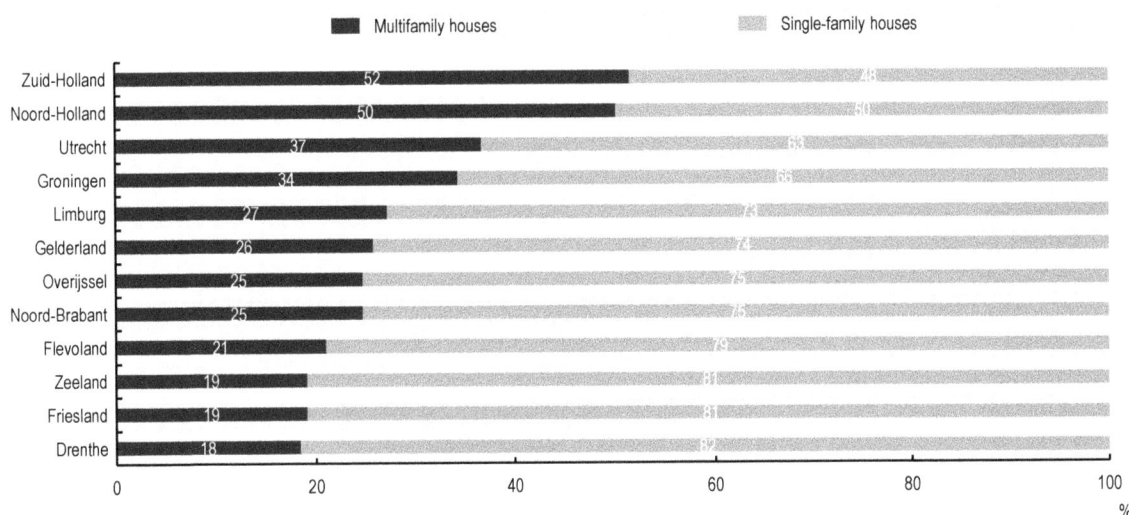

Source: Calculated based on the data provided by Ministry of the Interior and Kingdom Relations.

The share of multifamily housing and single-family housing in total housing stock varies significantly across regions in the Netherlands. The percentage of multifamily housing ranges from 18% in Drenthe to 52% in Zuid-Holland, reflecting the percentage of urban population (Figure 2.5).

Figure 2.5. Share of multifamily housing and single-family housing in the Netherlands by province

Source: Calculated based on the data provided by Ministry of the Interior and Kingdom Relations.

From an energy perspective, a higher share of multifamily housing reduces household energy consumption per capita. This is not only because multifamily housing is smaller in size than single-family housing, but also because its overall building structure makes the units more energy efficient (Obrinsky and Walter, 2016[15]). In the Netherlands, an average household living in a detached house consumes more than twice as much energy as a household in an apartment, in both natural gas and electricity (Figure 2.6).

Figure 2.6. Average energy consumption by type of dwelling in the Netherlands (per year)

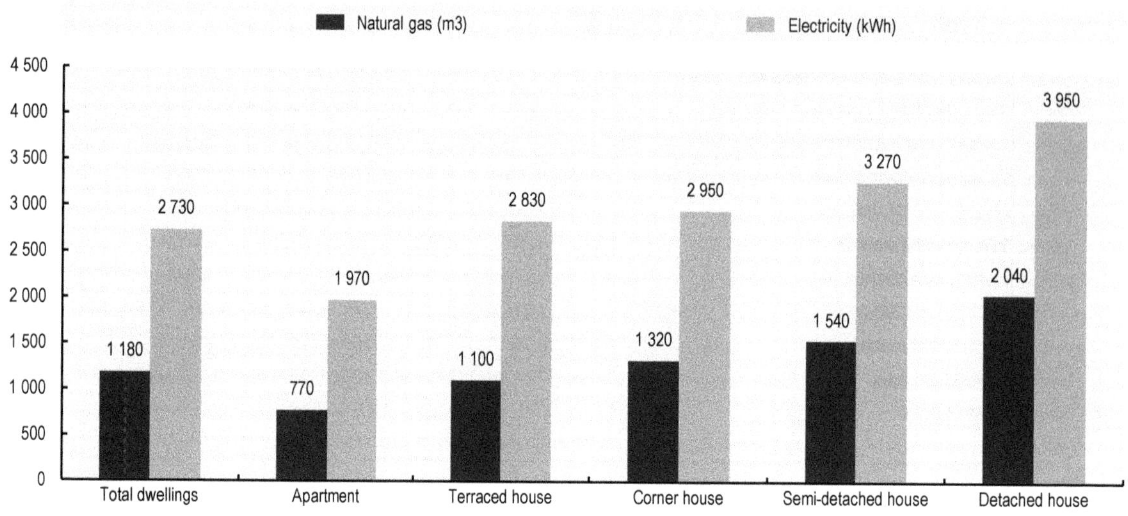

Legend: Natural gas (m3); Electricity (kWh)

Dwelling type	Natural gas (m3)	Electricity (kWh)
Total dwellings	1 180	2 730
Apartment	770	1 970
Terraced house	1 100	2 830
Corner house	1 320	2 950
Semi-detached house	1 540	3 270
Detached house	2 040	3 950

Source: Calculated based on the data provided by Ministry of the Interior and Kingdom Relations.

The rate of new construction and renovations is an important factor in designing and implementing policies, since they offer precious opportunities for energy efficiency measures. Energy efficiency investments are often much less costly in new construction than in renovations. The investment opportunity is high in regions with urban expansion, since the regions require a faster rate of new construction to accommodate population growth.

The rate of new construction differs greatly across regions in the Netherlands, ranging from 0.42% in Limburg to 1.06% in Flevoland. Although new construction does not necessarily replace old buildings, this indicator indicates to some extent the opportunities for comprehensive energy performance improvement in buildings. While new construction provides ample opportunities for local communities to modernise the built environment in regions with a higher construction rate, communities with a lower construction rate need to consider energy renovations more seriously (Figure 2.7).

Figure 2.7. Average new construction rate in the Netherlands by province (all buildings), 2012-20

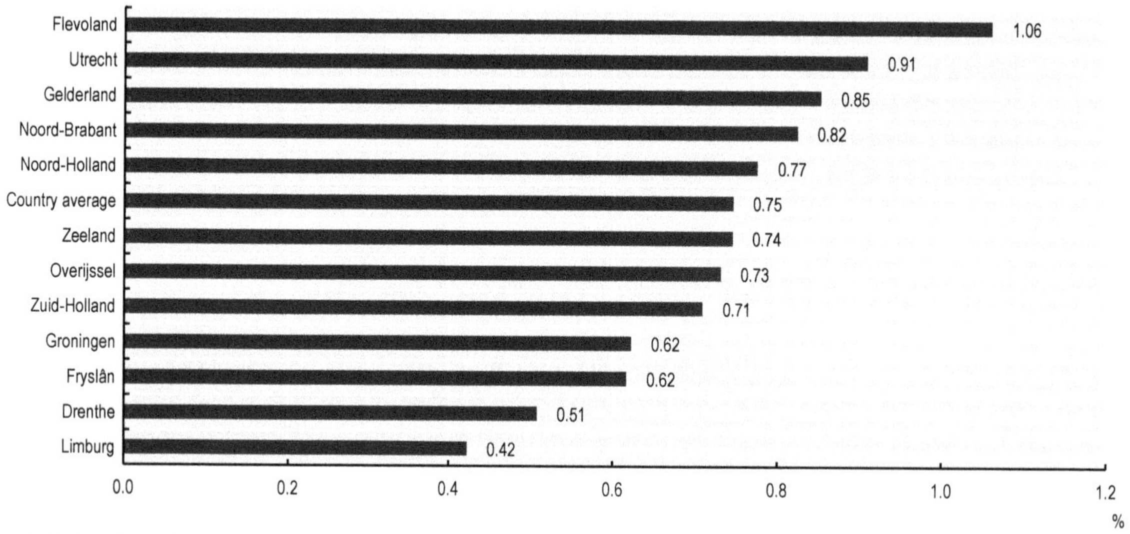

Province	%
Flevoland	1.06
Utrecht	0.91
Gelderland	0.85
Noord-Brabant	0.82
Noord-Holland	0.77
Country average	0.75
Zeeland	0.74
Overijssel	0.73
Zuid-Holland	0.71
Groningen	0.62
Fryslân	0.62
Drenthe	0.51
Limburg	0.42

Source: Calculated based on the data provided by Ministry of the Interior and Kingdom Relations.

Cities and regions face different policy environments

Policy environments vary across regions, in various dimensions, including the status of housing affordability and energy poverty, how prepared the construction industry is, and the enforcement and certification capacities of local institutions. All these factors, which vary locally, affect the effectiveness of policy implementation to promote energy efficiency in buildings.

- For example, housing affordability has increasingly attracted political attention, especially in large metropolitan areas. Policies to require energy efficiency in housing are known to place upward pressure on house prices, given their effect on construction and maintenance costs (OECD, 2021[8]). Cities and regions need to assess carefully how policies governing decarbonisation of buildings affect house prices and rents and provide measures to reduce the housing burden.
- Energy poverty requires specific attention of policy makers, providing assistance for energy retrofits to low-income households. In OECD countries, nearly 20% of low-income populations have difficulty heating their homes (OECD, 2021[8]). In Portugal, 19.4% of the population were unable to keep their homes warm in 2018; in response, the government has been developing a National Long-Term Strategy to Tackle Energy Poverty. The strategy plans to reduce energy poverty at the national, regional and local level by 1) increasing energy efficiency in homes; 2) reinforcing access to energy services; 3) sharing robust knowledge and access to information about energy use, in order to improve energy literacy; and 4) reducing the burden of energy consumption (IEA, 2021[16]).
- The skill levels and capacity of local construction and other relevant industries may limit the expansion of energy efficiency measures. Energy efficiency investments require a certain set of knowledge and skills, both in design and in construction. Cities and regions need to consider developing the skills of local actors, in collaboration with experts.
- Finally, in most cases, national governments design building energy codes and regulations, but their adoption and enforcement depend on local governments (EBC, 2021[17]). Local governments' capacity to enforce building energy codes also varies and affects the efficiency and credibility of building decarbonisation policies and the motivation of property owners. Cities and regions need to pursue efficient and effective enforcement, while national governments also play an important role in ensuring that enough enforcement capacity exists at the local level.

Cities and regions' self-assessment of their strengths and weaknesses on energy efficiency in buildings also varies significantly. While the "Volume of new construction/renovation" and "Administrative capacity of local authorities" are recognised as strengths by most cities and regions in the OECD-CoR survey (67% and 57%, respectively), other cities and regions consider them their weaknesses (24% and 29%). On the other hand, "House price and housing affordability" and "Energy price and energy affordability" are recognised as weaknesses by most cities and regions (62% and 67%), while other cities and regions recognise them as their strengths (5% and 14%). In the case of cost of energy, high electricity prices may encourage building owners and tenants to adopt energy-saving measures and make energy efficiency investments, while relatively high electricity prices by comparison with natural gas prices may also provide negative incentives. In countries where the cost of electricity and natural gas varies steeply, electrifying the heating system is an expensive option for cities. In the UK, for example, 23% of the electricity price derives from climate and social levies, as compared with only 2% for gas. Consumer prices for electricity are five times more expensive than for gas. This deters consumers from adopting electric heat pumps (Rosenow and Lowes, 2021[18]). "Volume of old building stock" and "Volume of social housing stock" are also recognised as weaknesses by over 40% of cities and regions (62% and 43%), while some cities and regions recognise them as their strengths (19% and 24%). This suggests significant potential for improving energy efficiency for such building and housing stock. "Location of universities and research institutes" and "Preparedness/skill of local construction firms" are recognised as strengths by almost half of cities and regions. Recognition of the preparedness of local industry varies widely, and there would be diversifying needs across cities and regions (Figure 2.8). As for "Preparedness/skill of local construction firms", 29% of cities and regions consider this a weakness.

Figure 2.8. Local specificities and unique contexts related to decarbonisation of buildings

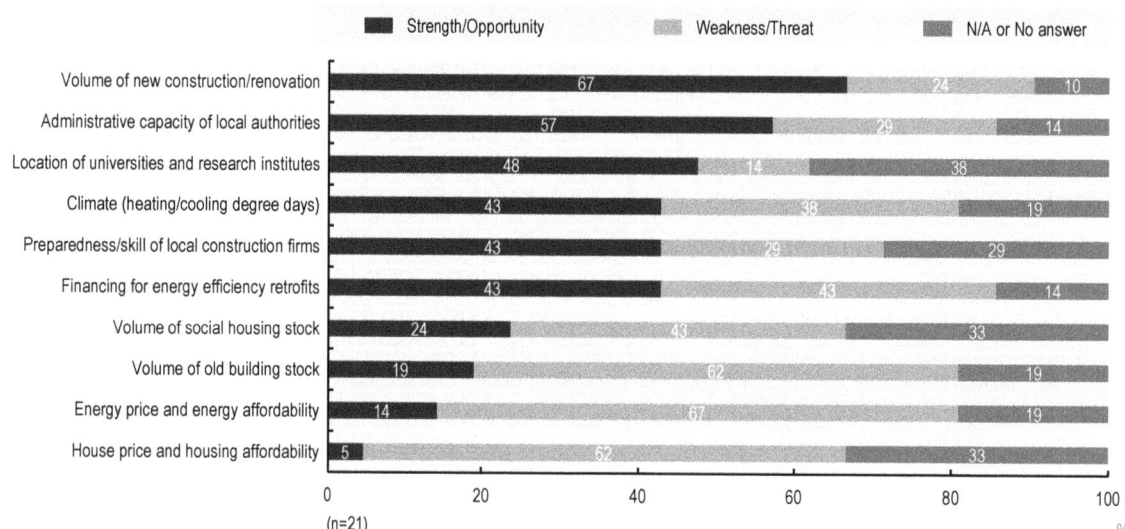

Source: OECD Survey on Decarbonising Buildings in Cities and Regions.

Decarbonisation of buildings offers multiple benefits at the local level

Energy efficiency improvements in buildings will generate multiple benefits, including job creation, health improvements and increased energy affordability, which will contribute to a green and inclusive recovery from COVID-19:

- **Job creation** (green growth, green recovery). The potential for job creation is estimated at from 9 to 30 jobs for every USD 1 million spent on energy efficiency measures in buildings (IEA, 2020[19]). In the EU, EUR 1 million investment in energy renovation of buildings is estimated to create 18 jobs on average (Renovate Europe, 2020[20]). In addition, these jobs are non-relocatable and include relatively low- to medium-skilled jobs, such as installation of insulation and window replacement in single-family homes, which can be accessed by unemployed workers (OECD, 2013[21]). The European Commission expects up to 160 000 additional green jobs to be created in the construction sector by 2030, by doubling renovation rates with its Renovation Wave Strategy (EC, 2020[22]).
- **Well-being** (health benefits, air pollution, etc.). In the EU, improving indoor air quality with enhanced energy efficiency measures and electrical equipment is estimated to save as much as USD 259 billion (EUR 190 billion) per year in savings in public health spending (IEA, 2014[23]). But the potential health benefits of energy efficiency improvements in buildings offer more than simply the cost savings. Measures to improve insulation, heating and ventilation enhance physical health, reducing symptoms of respiratory and cardiovascular conditions and improving mental health by reducing chronic stress and depression (IEA, 2019[24]). A Japanese survey of more than 2 000 houses and 4 000 occupants found that residents' blood pressure was significantly reduced after energy efficiency renovations, thanks to better indoor air temperature (MLIT, 2019[25]).

- **Energy affordability** (energy poor, etc.). Energy efficiency improvements in housing will also lead to increased energy affordability, especially among low-income households, even though the housing costs upfront could rise. For example, a study on Cincinnati's low-income weatherisation programme found that the average arrears of households that joined the programme fell by more than 60% after energy efficiency improvements (IEA, 2014[23]).

Cities and regions value social and environmental benefits of energy efficiency in buildings. The benefit most valued by the cities and regions that responded to the survey is "Reduced cost of paying the energy bill for low-income households" (rated very important by 89%), followed by "Reduction of greenhouse gas emissions" (84%), "Reduction of energy consumption and increased energy independence" (74%) and "Decreased air pollution" (63%) (Figure 2.9). Economic or well-being benefits such as "Job creation and economic competitiveness in green industries", "More comfortable and productive working spaces" and "More comfortable homes" are not considered as important, but they are rated at least moderately important by most cities and regions. Other benefits for cities include raising capacity of existing electrical grids and facilitating electrification, since the energy savings can be used to electrify high-efficiency home appliances, air-conditioners and electric vehicles (EV) without further increases in electricity consumption, in particular for peak loads, and upgrades in electricity production capacity (IEA, 2021[26]).

Figure 2.9. Primary benefits of energy efficiency in buildings recognised by cities and regions

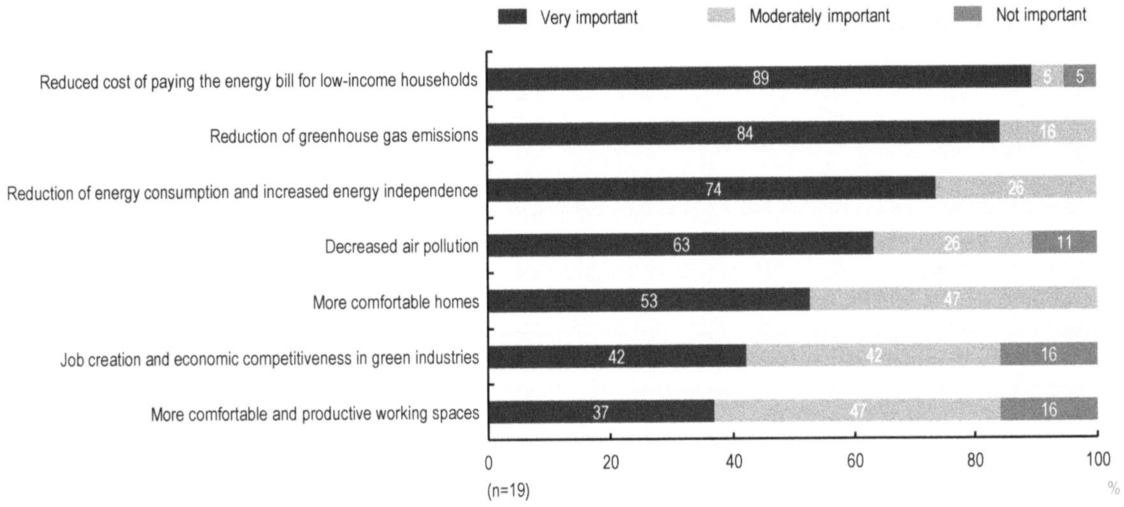

Benefit	Very important	Moderately important	Not important
Reduced cost of paying the energy bill for low-income households	89	5	5
Reduction of greenhouse gas emissions	84	16	
Reduction of energy consumption and increased energy independence	74	26	
Decreased air pollution	63	26	11
More comfortable homes	53	47	
Job creation and economic competitiveness in green industries	42	42	16
More comfortable and productive working spaces	37	47	16

(n=19)

Source: OECD Survey on Decarbonising Buildings in Cities and Regions.

References

City of Paris and Paris Climate Agency (2020), "Report of Paris greenhouse gas emissions in 2018", https://parisactionclimat.paris.fr/en/report-paris-greenhouse-gas-emissions-2018 (accessed on 30 October 2021). [4]

EBC (2021), *Building Energy Codes and Other Mandatory Policies Applied to Existing Buildings*, https://www.iea-ebc.org/Data/Sites/1/media/docs/working-groups/building-energy-codes/ebc_wg_becs_codesothermandatorypolicies-existingbuildings_june_2021.pdf (accessed on 29 January 2022). [17]

EC (2020), "Renovation wave: Doubling the renovation rate to cut emissions, boost recovery and reduce energy poverty", European Commission, https://ec.europa.eu/commission/presscorner/detail/en/ip_20_1835 (accessed on 15 November 2021). [22]

Erbach, G. (2015), "Understanding energy efficiency", https://www.europarl.europa.eu/RegData/etudes/BRIE/2015/568361/EPRS_BRI(2015)568361_EN.pdf. [14]

European Commission (2021), "Energy consumption in households", https://ec.europa.eu/eurostat/statistics-explained/index.php?title=Energy_consumption_in_households#Energy_products_used_in_the_residential_sector (accessed on 30 October 2021). [9]

Greater London Authority (2018), *London Environment Strategy*, https://www.london.gov.uk/sites/default/files/london_environment_strategy_0.pdf (accessed on 30 November 2020). [2]

IEA (2021), "Net zero by 2050 hinges on a global push to increase energy efficiency – Analysis", International Energy Agency, https://www.iea.org/articles/net-zero-by-2050-hinges-on-a-global-push-to-increase-energy-efficiency (accessed on 23 January 2022). [26]

IEA (2021), *Portugal 2021 Energy Policy Review*, International Energy Agency, https://iea.blob.core.windows.net/assets/a58d6151-f75f-4cd7-891e-6b06540ce01f/Portugal2021EnergyPolicyReview.pdf (accessed on 29 January 2022). [16]

IEA (2020), *Sustainable Recovery*, International Energy Agency, https://iea.blob.core.windows.net/assets/c3de5e13-26e8-4e52-8a67-b97aba17f0a2/Sustainable_Recovery.pdf (accessed on 15 November 2021). [19]

IEA (2019), *Multiple Benefits of Energy Efficiency: Health and Wellbeing*, International Energy Agency, https://www.iea.org/reports/multiple-benefits-of-energy-efficiency/health-and-wellbeing (accessed on 23 January 2022). [24]

IEA (2019), *The Critical Role of Buildings: Perspectives for the Clean Energy Transition*, International Energy Agency, http://www.iea.org/publications/reports/PerspectivesfortheCleanEnergyTransition/ (accessed on 23 October 2021). [1]

IEA (2018), *The Future of Cooling: Opportunities for Energy-efficient Air Conditioning*, International Energy Agency, https://iea.blob.core.windows.net/assets/0bb45525-277f-4c9c-8d0c-9c0cb5e7d525/The_Future_of_Cooling.pdf (accessed on 21 January 2022). [13]

IEA (2014), *Capturing the Multiple Benefits of Energy Efficiency: A Guide to Quantifying the Value Added*, International Energy Agency, https://doi.org/10.1787/9789264220720-en. (accessed on 30 November 2020). [23]

MLIT (2019), "The study on the impacts of energy efficiency renovations on the physical health of residents", Ministry of Land, Infrastructure, Transport and Tourism, https://www.mlit.go.jp/common/001270049.pdf (accessed on 30 November 2020). [25]

New York City Mayor's Office of Sustainability (2017), *1.5°C: Aligning New York City with the Paris Climate Agreement*, https://www1.nyc.gov/site/sustainability/codes/1.5-climate-action-plan.page (accessed on 23 October 2021). [5]

Obrinsky, M. and C. Walter (2016), "Energy Efficiency in Multifamily Rental Homes: An Analysis of Residential Energy Consumption Data", *Journal of Sustainable Real Estate*, Vol. 8/1, pp. 2-19, http://dx.doi.org/10.1080/10835547.2016.12091885 (accessed on 23 October 2021). [15]

OECD (2021), *Brick by Brick: Building Better Housing Policies*, OECD Publishing, Paris, https://doi.org/10.1787/b453b043-en. [8]

OECD (2021), *OECD Regional Outlook 2021: Addressing COVID-19 and Moving to Net Zero Greenhouse Gas Emissions*, OECD Publishing, Paris, https://dx.doi.org/10.1787/17017efe-en. [6]

OECD (2020), *OECD Regions and Cities at a Glance 2020*, OECD Publishing, Paris, https://dx.doi.org/10.1787/959d5ba0-en. [7]

OECD (2020), "The role of regions and cities towards a climate-neutral economy (SDG 13)", in *OECD Regions and Cities at a Glance 2020*, OECD Publishing, Paris, https://dx.doi.org/10.1787/6acbc792-en. [11]

OECD (2013), *Green Growth in Cities*, OECD Green Growth Studies, OECD Publishing, Paris, https://dx.doi.org/10.1787/9789264195325-en. [21]

OECD (n.d.), *OECD Metropolitan Database*, OECD, Paris, https://stats.oecd.org/Index.aspx?Datasetcode=CITIES. [12]

Renovate Europe (2020), "Building renovation: A kick-starter for the EU economy", https://www.renovate-europe.eu/2020/06/10/building-renovation-a-kick-starter-for-the-eu-economy/ (accessed on 15 November 2021). [20]

Rosenow, J. and R. Lowes (2021), "Redesigning UK electricity taxes to boost Heat Pump sales", *Energypost.eu*, https://energypost.eu/redesigning-uk-electricity-taxes-to-boost-heat-pump-sales/ (accessed on 23 January 2022). [18]

Tokyo Metropolitan Government Bureau of Environment (2018), *Final Energy Consumption and Greenhouse Gas Emissions in Tokyo (FY2015)*, http://www.kankyo.metro.tokyo.jp/en/climate/index.files/GHG2015.pdf (accessed on 30 November 2020). [3]

U.S. Energy Information Administration (2021), *Use of Energy Explained: Energy Use in Homes*, https://www.eia.gov/energyexplained/use-of-energy/homes.php (accessed on 30 October 2021). [10]

3 What are cities and regions doing to decarbonise buildings?

This chapter analyses the four main roles and actions of cities and regions in decarbonising buildings: 1) regulations; 2) financing; 3) planning and co-ordination; and 4) engagement of local actors, based on the results from the OECD Survey on Decarbonising Cities and Regions. Cities and regions are undertaking ambitious policy measures on building energy codes and public buildings, which can be scaled up. Support for financing could be further diversified to meet the needs of property owners with locally available resources. Most cities and regions surveyed have their own plans, but face challenges in implementing them, such as incomplete monitoring and evaluation. Subnational governments already promote citizen engagement and can expand private sector engagement and support for local industry.

Decarbonising buildings, in particular existing buildings, requires a comprehensive set of policy measures. A single policy instrument cannot fully address the variety of barriers that building owners face in making the decision to invest in building decarbonisation. These include high upfront costs; lack of consumer awareness; and high transaction costs (e.g. lengthy negotiation processes with renters, co-owners and a wide array of service providers). A variety of policy instruments are available, including regulations (e.g. mandatory building energy codes); financial incentives (e.g. grants, tax exemptions, low-interest loans and mortgages, and small-scale financing); awareness raising and information provision (e.g. building energy performance certification); and stakeholder engagement. However, an individual policy instrument does not appear to create an incentive great enough for property owners to invest in building decarbonisation. A comprehensive policy mix that combines these measures is clearly needed, as well as planning and implementation that create larger impacts.

National policies play a key role in setting up a framework for energy efficiency investments and providing supporting policy instruments to incentivise property owners and developers. These include stricter building energy codes for both new and existing buildings, mandatory energy performance certificates for buildings for sale or rent, and tax incentives for renovations. On the other hand, cities and regions have a unique ability to promote the decarbonisation of building stock by devising their own regulatory and financial policy measures, as well as by promoting effective planning and stakeholder engagement that is tailored to local needs. This section analyses the key role of cities and regions and assesses cities and regions' progress on four key aspects of building decarbonisation that are particularly relevant for cities and regions: 1) regulatory tools and frameworks; 2) financing and business models; 3) planning and co-ordination; and 4) engagement and skill development of local actors.

Leveraging regulatory tools and frameworks for building decarbonisation

Regulations are the most fundamental policy tools for improving buildings' energy efficiency. A wide array of regulations can be used, including mandatory building energy codes, strict requirements for public buildings or buildings on public land, restrictions on the sale and rent of the worst-performing buildings and carbon emission caps for large buildings. The challenge is how to develop ambitious, effective regulatory measures that can drive energy efficiency improvements in existing buildings in order to achieve net-zero carbon building stock, while ensuring both housing affordability and effective enforcement of these regulations. The key step is to engage and support cities and regions in this process effectively, since they are familiar with local building stock and, in most cases, responsible for zoning and code enforcement. Some cities are even introducing their own original ambitious regulations. In addition, subnational governments own a large number of public buildings, for example public housing, government offices, public schools and community centres. It is cities and regions that can impose a higher standard of energy efficiency requirements for public buildings and that can encourage new technologies and business models for further renovations in private buildings.

Building energy codes and other regulations

Building energy codes are a key instrument for ensuring the construction and maintenance of energy efficient buildings. However, the coverage of building energy codes is rarely uniformly applied and, where they are in place, the codes may not be aligned with the goal of net-zero carbon emissions by 2050. In November 2021, building energy codes were in place in 80 countries, of which only 54 countries had mandatory codes at the national level for both residential and non-residential buildings (IEA, 2021[1]). Sub-Saharan Africa and South and Central America have the least widespread coverage of mandatory codes. These codes are mandatory in most developed countries, although whether they are mandatory also varies by region in some countries. In addition, an increasing number of countries and regions have introduced building energy certification (UNEP, 2021[2]). Of the cities and regions that responded to the

OECD survey, 89% have building energy codes in place, of which 71% are mandatory. It can be assumed that the overall percentages are lower, given that those that responded to the OECD survey are likely to be more aware and engaged in the agenda for decarbonising buildings. A key challenge for policy makers is to broaden the coverage and enforcement of mandatory building energy codes across all local and regional governments, especially including those in developing economies. Enforcement of building energy codes is important, as the actual energy performance of buildings depends on their compliance with the building energy codes. It will fall to municipalities, which are often responsible for carrying out on-site inspections and issuing building permits, to check them effectively.

Another key challenge is how to apply the requisite level of energy efficiency requirements to existing buildings. Of the 17 cities and regions with building energy codes in place, whether mandatory or voluntary, 35% apply building energy codes only to new buildings (Figure 3.1). Given the very low rate of new construction (about 0.5-2% in developed economies), regulations have very small impacts on the energy performance of the overall building stock. Some cities and regions also apply building energy codes to existing buildings, including the region of Emilia-Romagna (Italy), Scania province (Sweden), Toronto (Canada) and Oakland (US). Most cities and regions apply building energy codes when building owners undertake renovations at a certain scale. Scania province applies them to all existing buildings and Emilia-Romagna applies them when buildings are rented or sold.

Figure 3.1. Primary targets for building energy codes applied in cities and regions

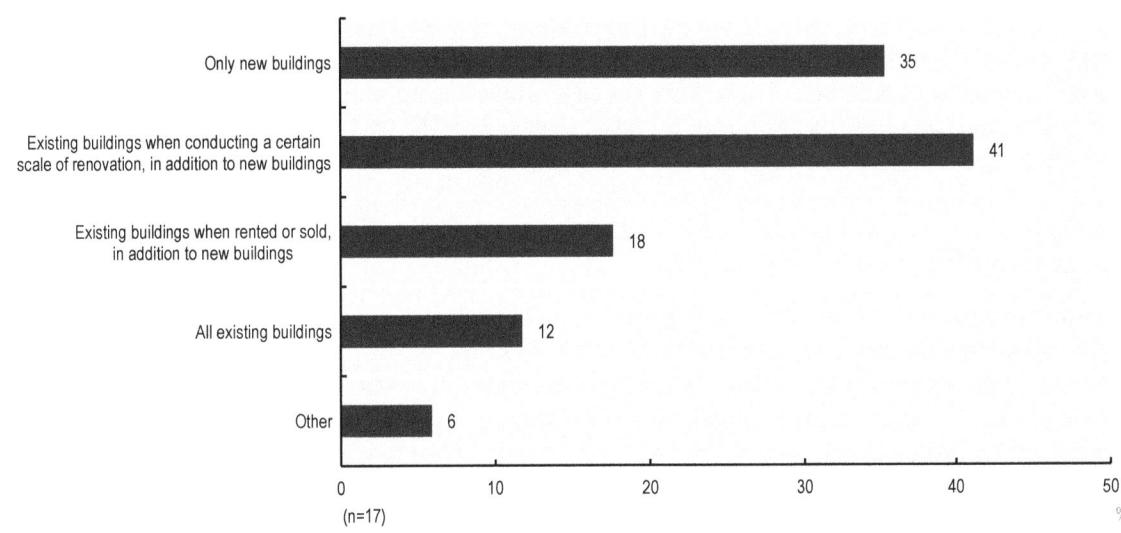

Source: OECD Survey on Decarbonising Buildings in Cities and Regions.

While many cities and regions apply national building energy codes or equivalent codes, 53% of cities and regions that responded to the survey have their own building energy codes. Most cities and regions (88%) require higher energy efficiency than national building energy codes and 25% require buildings to be net-zero energy level. For example, the cities of Stockholm and Toronto require a much higher level of energy efficiency than their national building energy codes do. In the case of Scania province, building energy codes require the level of net-zero-energy buildings for new buildings and part of existing buildings. This indicates that the potential subnational governments have to develop more ambitious building energy codes. Considering that a disproportionate percentage of population and buildings are concentrated in cities, large, high-income cities with more human and technical resources can play a key role in spearheading ambitious regulations. When applying ambitious building energy codes, such as net-zero energy level, cities and regions also need to provide a road map to allow lead time for the relevant industries to explore cost-optimal ways of achieving net zero. For instance, in Canada, the Province of

British Columbia has taken the initiative to bring multiple stakeholders and cities together and successfully introduced its innovative province-wide building energy codes, BC Step Code, to achieve zero-energy buildings by 2032 (Box 3.1). When applying these high-level building energy codes to renovations, cities and regions also need to define a timetable for buildings, to make sure that renovation work can be sequenced and bundled in order to minimise costs.

In addition to building energy codes, cities and regions have introduced a variety of regulatory measures capitalising on their jurisdiction over buildings and their interactions with property owners. These include zoning regulations, stricter energy efficiency requirements on public land, mandatory building certification, mandatory reporting of energy consumption or carbon emissions, and mandatory emissions caps. Some cities are introducing stricter and more ambitious standards for building energy efficiency than those at the national level. Stockholm, for example, has introduced a Passive House Standard (a maximum of 55 kWh/m^2) for new construction on city-owned land, higher than the national standard (80 kWh/m^2) (Eurocities, 2019[3]). New York City has introduced an ambitious regulation requiring existing buildings of more than 25 000 square feet to cap their greenhouse gas emissions starting in 2024. The city aims to reduce emissions from buildings in line with climate targets based on its past efforts, including mandatory disclosure of the energy demand of large buildings and advisory services for energy efficiency retrofits (New York City Mayor's Office of Sustainability, 2019[4]).

Box 3.1. Net-zero energy-ready buildings through shared leadership: British Columbia, Canada

Background and problem: To achieve net-zero carbon emission by 2050 at the least cost, all new buildings must be so-called net-zero energy buildings. Introducing ambitious building energy codes is not an easy task, however, since building value chains need to be prepared for the new modes of construction, and universal coverage in a region is needed to encourage a transformation of the market. In British Columbia, incremental revisions to the provincial building energy codes and fragmented applications of different local codes were holding back effective low-carbon transition in the building sector, as is often the case in other regions.

Innovative solutions: The province of British Columbia solved this problem by taking the initiative to bring multiple stakeholders and cities together and introduce innovative province-wide building energy codes. The Energy Step Code provides a roadmap for required levels of building energy performance, allowing gradual interim steps to reach net-zero energy level (20% improvement by 2022, 40% improvement by 2027 and net-zero energy ready by 2032). It clarifies goals for business planning and lead time for builders and manufacturers to explore more energy efficient technologies, practices and products. British Columbia has also created the Energy Step Code Council, a multi-stakeholder advisory body of representatives from provincial ministries, major industry and professional associations, covering more than 55 000 members in the province. The Council has developed implementation guidelines on the Energy Step Code and provided support for both local businesses and municipalities. It also helped small municipalities with less technical capacities to prepare for the next steps.

Impacts and benefits: The share of new residential construction subject to the Energy Step Code has increased to 70% in 2019, from 22% in 2018. In addition, preparedness in both municipalities and business sector has increased at a rapid rate. The percentage of local governments rated as having "moderate, good or excellent knowledge of the BC Step Code" increased to 88% in 2019 from 61% in 2017, while the share of businesses reporting "feeling prepared for BC Energy Step Code" exceeded 70% in 2019. It is estimated that Vancouver's green building policies and other local governments' implementation of the Energy Step Code will create a CAD 3.3 billion market for green building products and about 1 700 jobs each year for Metro Vancouver from 2019 to 2032. By 2030, including the impacts by the Energy Step Code, the province of British Columbia aims to reduce greenhouse gas (GHG) emissions by 40% below 2007 levels.

Experience and lessons: First, to create a momentum for a market transformation, regional governments can develop long-term roadmaps towards ambitious targets (e.g. net-zero energy level) for both industry and local communities, rather than taking the traditional, short-term approach of adding incremental improvements to the code. Second, regional governments can create a platform for a wide range of stakeholders, using their networks to provide technical support to businesses and communities in need. This will help to introduce an ambitious regional vision, despite the variations in preparedness and skill levels within a region.

Source: BC Housing (2020[5]), *2019 BC Energy Step Code Market Response Study*, https://energystepcode.ca/reports/ (accessed on 23 October 2021); BC Housing's Research Centre and the Community Energy Association (2019[6]), *2019 BC Energy Step Code Local Government Survey*, https://energystepcode.ca/app/uploads/sites/257/2019/07/FINAL-BC-Energy-Step-Code-Local-Government-Survey-Report-July-2019.pdf; Government of British Columbia (n.d.[7]), *Energy Step Code*, https://energystepcode.ca/; Glave, J. and R. Wark (Glave and Wark, 2019[8]), *Lessons from the BC Energy Step Code*, https://www2.gov.bc.ca/assets/gov/farming-natural-resources-and-industry/construction-industry/building-codes-and-standards/reports/bcenergystepcode_lessons_learned_final.pdf (accessed on 23 October 2021); Vancouver Economic Commission (2019[9]), *Green Buildings Market Forecast: Demand for Building Products, Metro Vancouver 2019–2032*, https://www.vancouvereconomic.com/research/green-buildings-market-research/ (accessed on 23 October 2021); May, Z. (2020[10]), "Energy Step Code – Building Beyond the Standard", https://www.oecd.org/cfe/cities/energy-efficiency-cities.htm; Energy Step Code (n.d.[11]), *About the site and council*, https://energystepcode.ca/about/.

Public building policies

Subnational governments own a large number of public buildings, such as public housing, government offices, public schools and community centres. Cities and regions can impose a higher level of energy efficiency requirements for public buildings and encourage new technologies and business models for further renovations in private buildings.

No comprehensive and internationally comparable database exists with information on the volume and breakdown of non-residential building stock. However, from national renovation strategies or websites of national statistical offices, it appears that subnational buildings account for an extremely large portion of this building stock. For example, in the Czech Republic, public buildings account for 29% of the total non-residential building stock in terms of floor area and 19% in terms of the number of buildings. Because public buildings include relatively large facilities, such as libraries, museum and sports facilities, the cities' and regions' share in terms of floor area is higher than their share in terms of the number of buildings. Among public buildings, national government buildings account for only 4% in floor area and 2% in number, and subnational buildings account for remaining 24% in floor area and 17% in number. In particular, relatively small municipalities with populations of less than 50 000 account for 17% in floor area, while larger municipalities with populations of more than 50 000 account for 7% (Ministry of Industry and Trade, 2020[12]). Similarly, public buildings in France account for about 37% of non-residential building stock, of which the central government and its agencies own 10% (100 million square metres [m²]) and regional and local authorities own 20% (208 million m²) (Government of France, 2020[13]). In Japan, subnational buildings account for about 30% (600 million m²) of all non-residential building stock (2 billion m²), while the central government owns only 2% (44 million m²) (MLIT, 2018[14]). In sum, subnational buildings account for a very large portion of non-residential building stock, although this may vary across countries. Cities and regions should prioritise decarbonisation of their own building stock and use it as a catalyst for decarbonisation of buildings more broadly.

Almost all cities and regions (95%) that responded to the OECD survey promote energy efficiency measures for public buildings. In most cities and regions, the targeted buildings are offices and educational facilities. Some cities and regions, however, also target healthcare facilities, public housing, medical facilities and other facilities such as libraries, community centres and sports facilities. The types of energy efficiency measures taken for public buildings are quite diverse. "Energy efficiency renovations/retrofits" and "Renewable energy use" were the most popular measures cited by the cities and regions participating the survey. On the other hand, "Digital technologies", such as smart efficient buildings, grid-interactive buildings and smart meters, are only cited by a third of cities and regions that promote energy efficiency measures for public buildings. As for the level of energy efficiency required for public buildings, of the 18 cities and regions that responded to the question, 28% require a much higher level of energy efficiency for public buildings and 33% require slightly higher levels, while other cities and regions require the same or lower levels of energy efficiency or levels that cannot be compared with nationally required levels (Figure 3.2). 27% require the level of net-zero energy building for public buildings. In particular, Scania province requires it for part of existing buildings in addition to new buildings. On the other hand, the City of Toronto requires a net-zero feasibility study for all building retrofits and new constructions, including evaluation of renewable energy potential.

Figure 3.2. Percentage of cities and regions whose public buildings require greater energy efficiency than national levels

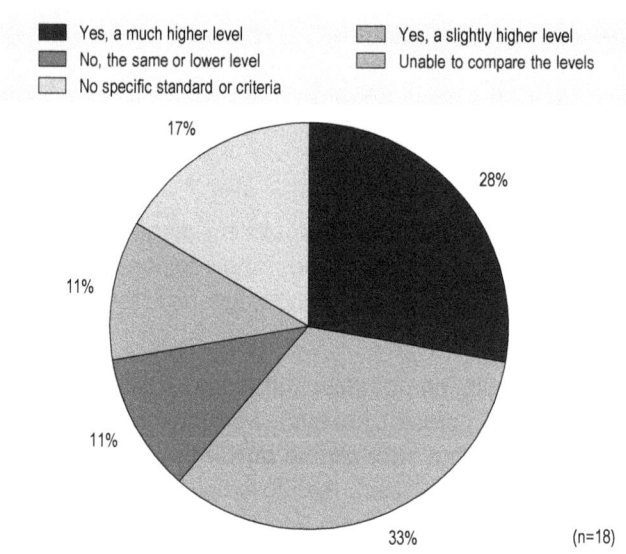

Source: OECD Survey on Decarbonising Buildings in Cities and Regions.

Cities can utilise their investment in public buildings (and subsidized housing) to achieve better energy performance in buildings. In 2006, Geneva (Switzerland) adopted the strategy "100% renewable by 2050", in response to increasing oil prices and its energy dependence on fossil fuels. By identifying buildings that would benefit from renovation from an energy and environmental perspective, the energy performance of municipal buildings has increased (Energycities, 2016[15]). In Austria, the city of Vienna launched a competition among developers making tenders for construction of subsidized residential housing, to develop affordable and energy efficient timber housing (Energycities, 2020[16]). Investment in public buildings can be used to require a higher standard of energy performance, as well as to explore new technologies and offer learning opportunities for local construction firms.

Supporting financing and business models for energy renovation

Financing is another key element in scaling up energy efficiency investment in buildings, since it requires a significant amount of costs upfront. A variety of financial incentives can be used, including tax breaks, low-interest rate mortgages and grants. It appears, however, that these incentives are not enough to persuade individual property owners to invest in energy efficiency renovations at the required pace to achieve net-zero carbon building stock by 2050. Together with stricter regulations, effective financing schemes are urgently needed to fully incentivise property owners to invest in deep energy retrofits as well as to reduce the burden of these regulations, especially on vulnerable households. In the context of green recovery from COVID-19, many cities and regions plan to invest in energy efficiency in both new and existing buildings, which will generate local jobs.

National recovery packages and supranational initiatives, including the European Renovation Wave, present vast opportunities for subnational governments to promote decarbonisation of their own public buildings as well as private building stocks in their areas. The European Commission (EC) estimated that the Renovation Wave initiative will renovate up to 35 million buildings and create 160 000 additional jobs in the construction sector in Europe by 2030 (EC, 2020[17]). Cities and regions can take the lead in deep energy renovations of public buildings, promote and aggregate local renovation needs and bring in key stakeholders to develop financing schemes and business models. In Canada, British Columbia has a financing mechanism, the Clean BC Better Homes Low-Interest Financing Program, to provide loans at a promotional interest rate of 0% for switching from a heating system with fossil fuel (oil, propane or natural gas) to a heat pump (Clean BC, n.d.[18]). British Columbia's Energy Conservation Assistance Program targets low-income households and provides an in-home visit with free energy-saving product installation, including energy-saving LED light bulbs, high-efficiency showerheads and weather-stripping to reduce drafts. Similarly, in 2022, the city of Toronto is expected to launch an enhanced Home Energy Loan Program to offer loans of up to CAD 125 000, with interest rates as low as 0%, to homeowners who are planning to cover the cost of home energy improvements (City of Toronto, n.d.[19]). Of 20 cities and regions that responded to the questions in the OECD survey on financing, 65% reported having their own financial incentives or financing mechanisms. This percentage is quite high, considering that energy efficiency policies have usually been conceived of as a national policy. "Renewable energy use", "Energy efficiency renovations/retrofits in general" and "Energy efficiency renovations/retrofits for low-income households" are the most popular measures that cities and regions support (69%, 62% and 54% respectively), before "Energy efficiency appliances and equipment", "District-scale energy management system", "Construction of energy efficient buildings" and "Digital technologies". High percentages for renewables and renovations reflect the limited opportunities for taking a wide array of measures, such as in new construction and the focus of these cities and regions on existing buildings. The most popular financial tools among cities and regions are "Grants" (69% of cities and regions that have their own financial incentives or financing mechanisms), "Promotion of new business models" (31%) and "Loans and loan guarantees" (23%). Other forms of financing, such as "Auctions and (energy company) obligations" and "Small-scale financing" are not used in the cities and regions that responded to the survey (Figure 3.3).

Although they can be ambitious, ongoing policy actions, including financial incentives, cannot by themselves promote energy efficiency investment to achieve net-zero carbon emissions by 2050 in the building sector. Experimental pilot projects are also needed to promote innovative business models encouraging property owners to alleviate the distributional impacts of climate policies, particularly on low-income households. Energy efficiency retrofits for these families need to be supported. As for pilot projects, the Netherlands has launched its Programme for Natural Gas-Free Neighbourhoods, a district-oriented approach aiming to help 1.5 million homes transition from gas to low-carbon heating by 2030 (IEA, 2020[20]). The programme promotes knowledge sharing between municipalities and selects pilot areas for districts free of natural gas. The selected pilot projects receive around EUR 4 million from the national government to help cover the financing gap for the full investment. The goal is to have 100 pilot areas by 2028 (PAW, n.d.[21]).

Figure 3.3. Financing tools used in cities and regions

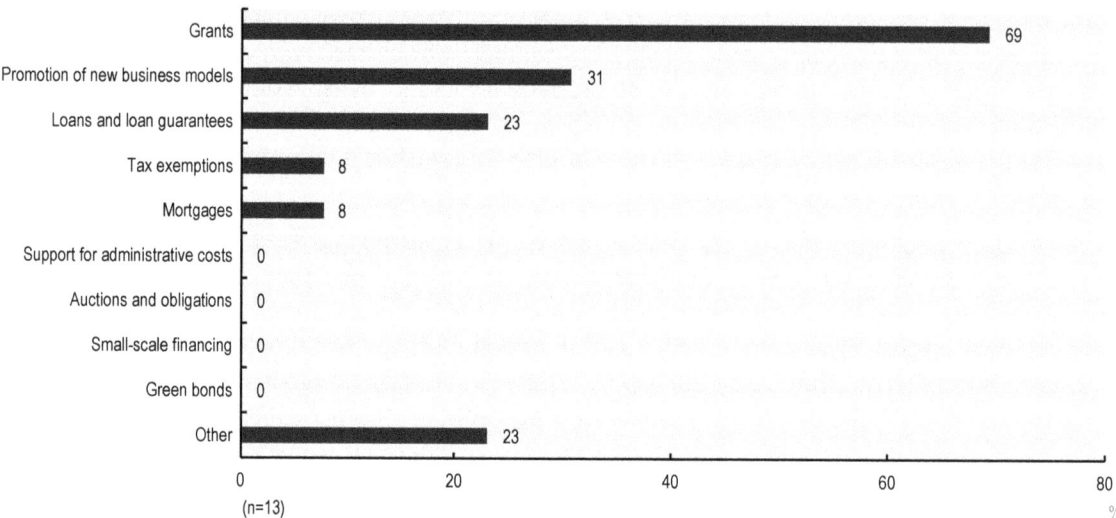

Source: OECD Survey on Decarbonising Buildings in Cities and Regions.

To promote new business models, cities and regions can take advantage of public building investment and bundle dispersed renovation needs, to create markets of sufficient size for private investment. This may lead to mass application of low-cost production technologies and increased financial opportunities for renovations. The *Energiesprong* programme in the Netherlands is an innovative example that consolidated social housing renovation needs and achieved net-zero energy renovations in more than 5 000 homes (Energiesprong Foundation, n.d.[22]) (Box 3.2). Similarly, cities and regions can partner with companies that deploy innovative technologies. For instance, energy solutions promoted by Knauf, a European energy solution company, have contributed to social housing renovation in Belgium, with its technology measuring, hour by hour, the real energy and CO_2 savings of a retrofitted house. Using its negaWatt hour meter – which measures each unit of energy saved per hour as a direct result of energy conservation measures – it has documented energy-saving benefits that enable governments and private investors to monetise long-term energy savings and invest in renovation measures upfront (Knauf Insulation, 2021[23]).

Box 3.2. Energiesprong programme: Net-zero energy housing through energy renovations

The *Energiesprong* programme in the Netherlands is an innovative example that consolidated dispersed renovation needs and achieved net-zero energy renovations in more than 5 000 homes. It has also been tested in France, the United Kingdom and the state of New York. By bundling renovation needs in social housing and creating sufficient market size for private investment, it led to mass application of low-cost production technologies and increased financial opportunities. Using new technologies, such as prefabricated facades, insulated roofs with solar panels, smart heating and ventilation, it aims to complete renovation within 10 days and to ensure a long-term performance warranty on energy performance. These renovations, moreover, do not incur extra costs for residents, since they are financed by future energy cost savings and the budget for planned maintenance and repair costs for 30 years.

> The key lesson of this initiative is that the programme has brought together multiple stakeholders (e.g. the construction industry, housing authorities, financial institutions and energy utilities) and provided a comprehensive policy package for deep energy efficiency renovations of existing buildings. It includes negotiation between these key stakeholders and regulators on how to create enabling environments to start pilot projects and invest in off-site mass production, such as reviewing necessary legislative changes to allow new types of business models. A recent study noted the critical role of the market development team in the *Energiesprong* initiative as an intermediary promoting innovation to rethink the established systems of construction and contract design in energy efficiency retrofits. Innovations include helping to create standard processes for energy performance contracts, influencing procurement policies and volume agreements with public housing providers, and negotiating changes in regulations to allow placement of energy service charges on rents (Brown, Kivimaa and Sorrell, 2019[24]).
>
> The results of the *Energiesprong* programme have yet to be evaluated. After the initial government funding, the intention was that the programme should find market solutions to finance itself. The investment costs still range from about EUR 70 000 to more than EUR 100 000 per residential unit, while the estimated cost for a feasible business case would be about EUR 40 000 (Visscher, 2020[25]). The initiative is currently supported by the EU, national governments and local authorities, and is not yet viable without public subsidies. In addition, the model would face greater challenges in the owner-occupied housing market, since the diversity of building types would make mass production solutions more difficult. However, this innovative initiative can be instructive in encouraging systemic innovation in the built environment.
>
> Source: Brown, D., P. Kivimaa and S. Sorrell (2019[24]), "An energy leap? Business model innovation and intermediation in the 'Energiesprong' retrofit initiative", https://doi.org/10.1016/j.erss.2019.101253 (accessed on 23 October 2021); Energiesprong Foundation (n.d.[22]), *Energiesprong*, https://energiesprong.org/ (accessed on 30 November 2020; Visscher, H. (2020[25]), "Innovations for a carbon free Dutch housing stock in 2050", http://dx.doi.org/10.1088/1755-1315/588/3/032050; EC (2017[26]), "Netherlands, Energiesprong (Energy Leap)", https://ec.europa.eu/docsroom/documents/30290/attachments/3/translations/en/renditions/pdf (accessed on 23 October 2021).

Creating locally plans and strategies tailored to local needs

Planning and co-ordination are critical for energy efficiency policies in buildings. They need a comprehensive set of policy tools, engagement of a broad array of stakeholders and consideration of the local building stock. National governments in EU countries usually offer a country-wide vision and targets in their national climate and energy or building-specific plans, such as national long-term renovation strategies. However, the degree to which national plans take into account territorial disparities and subnational policy actions varies. In addition, policy coherence across levels of government is required to drive decarbonisation. Considering locally varying building stocks and policy environments, and their respective success in factoring in local elements and engaging citizens and local businesses, it is vital to engage subnational governments and integrate their policy actions into national plans. For example, in the United States, a myriad actions are taken across levels of government. At a federal level, Section 432 of the Energy Independence and Security Act of 2007 (EISA 432) requires energy evaluation of each covered facility every four years, to identify potential energy efficiency measures. To explore this potential, federal agencies are required to report annual building benchmarking requirements (EERE, n.d.[27]). Local governments adjust local conditions to tackle climate change and decarbonising buildings. On a city level, the city of San Francisco has passed its Existing Commercial Buildings Energy Performance Ordinance to benchmark and disclose building energy performance annually. The city and county of San Francisco began by benchmarking its municipal building energy use (SFWPS, n.d.[28]). Under the San Francisco Climate Action Plan 2021 (CAP), this energy benchmarking law motivated 3 114 large commercial and multifamily buildings to improve energy efficiency performance, reducing commercial energy use by 10%

between 2013 and 2017 (SF Environment, 2021[29]). Similarly, Paris has made city-specific building data publicly available to facilitate building renovation. Its digital map, known as EnerSIG, gives citizens building-related information at the neighbourhood level, including the number of residential units and buildings, when buildings were built, energy performance and heating systems (APUR, 2021[30]).

The OECD survey enquired whether subnational governments have their own plans or strategies for energy efficiency in buildings. Of the 21 cities and regions that responded, 86% have plans or strategies for energy efficiency in buildings, whether stand-alone, part of energy plans or part of climate plans. A majority have stand-alone plans or strategies on energy efficiency in buildings and have some components of energy efficiency in buildings in energy and climate plans. On the other hand, only 10% of the cities and regions surveyed included energy efficiency in buildings as part of their COVID-19 recovery plans or strategies (Figure 3.4). Of the cities and regions that have any kind of plans or strategies on energy efficiency in buildings, 82% have both quantitative targets and monitoring indicators. The targets vary in types, from the amount or percentage of buildings that should meet some sustainability standards to actual savings or reductions in energy consumption or CO_2 emissions.

Figure 3.4. Plans and strategies for energy efficiency in buildings

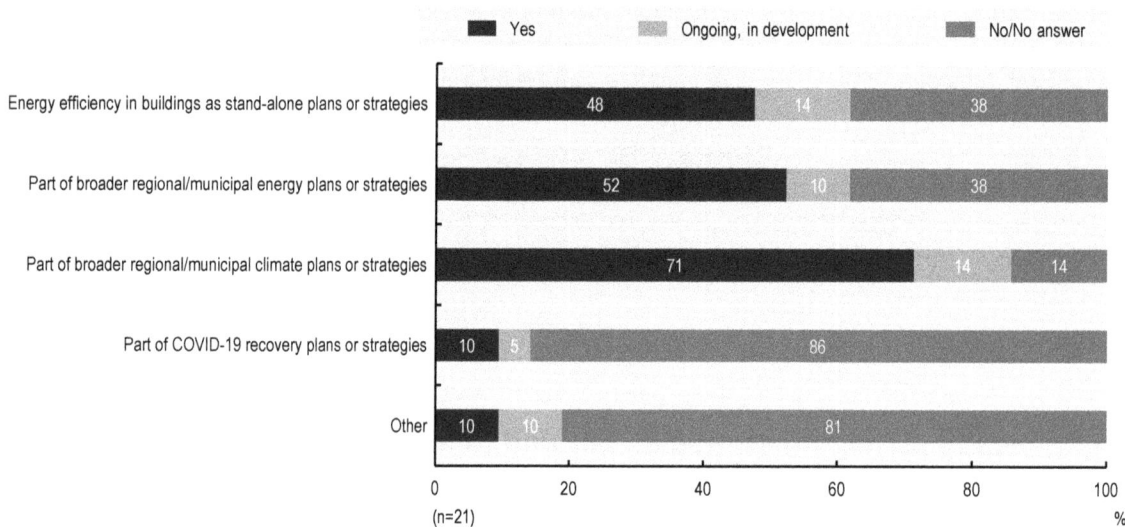

Source: OECD Survey on Decarbonising Buildings in Cities and Regions.

Energy efficiency plans or strategies developed at the local or regional level still face many challenges. One is that most quantitative targets are output-based, such as the number of housing units considered to be sustainable, or the percentage of buildings that conform to certain sustainability standards. It is easy for cities and regions to follow these quantitative targets and monitor progress. However, it is not so clear how much impact achieving these targets will have on reducing energy consumption or carbon emissions from buildings. On the other hand, when cities develop outcome-based indicators, for example, for the percentage of energy savings, they do not usually have monitoring indicators specifically connected to energy efficiency in buildings. Energy outcomes depend not only on energy efficiency policies but on such factors as weather conditions, energy prices and total floor area. Energy and carbon outcomes (e.g. energy consumption and carbon emissions from buildings) need to be tracked to evaluate policy outcomes against their targets. At the same time, cities and regions also need to monitor energy and carbon intensity (e.g. energy consumption and carbon emissions from buildings per m²) and the energy performance of buildings (e.g. a grade based on energy performance certification) to evaluate how policies have affected the energy performance of building stock. Of the survey respondents that have plans in place, 54% incorporate these targets in the municipal/regional investment planning process to identify or prioritise the municipal/regional investments. This is done in a variety of ways, including 1) monitoring policy progress (e.g. the number of housing units that a local programme supports, and the resulting GHG emissions), and 2) reflecting targets or failure to reach targets and present status in subnational budgets or strategic plans. This process is critical. Simply setting targets and a list of policy instruments does not ensure that the targets are achieved. Annual or biannual evaluation of policy progress and achievement of targets, and adjusting policy instruments and investment planning, appear to be an equally important condition for success.

In planning and implementing energy efficiency policies in buildings, most cities and regions recognise "Broader engagement of citizens and the private sector/greater awareness raising" (57%), "Greater support to innovative local projects and initiatives" (38%) and "Stricter building energy codes/minimum legal requirement" (38%) as their key priorities (Figure 3.5). About a quarter of cities and regions recognised "Greater capacity-building effort in subnational governments" (24%), "New or enhanced database on energy efficiency in buildings" (24%) and "Active co-operation to national policy implementation" (24%) as their key priorities. In particular, most mid-sized cities surveyed stress greater capacity building as one of their key priorities. National governments should better understand which types of cities and regions need particular support in capacity building to tailor their measures to place-based needs.

Figure 3.5. Key priorities of cities and regions on energy efficiency in buildings

Priority	%
Broader engagement of citizens and the private sector/greater awareness raising	57
Greater support to innovative local projects and initiatives	38
Stricter building energy codes/minimum legal requirement	38
Greater capacity building effort in subnational governments	24
New or enhanced database on energy efficiency in buildings	24
Active co-operation in national policy implementation	24
New or updated subnational plan or strategy on buildings	14
Greater support to technology development	10
Greater use of public building procurement	5
Other	33

(n=21)

Source: OECD Survey on Decarbonising Buildings in Cities and Regions.

Engaging and training local actors

Energy efficient buildings generate multiple benefits, including job creation, improved health and energy affordability. While experts and policy makers recognise these benefits and have designed their COVID-19 recovery packages accordingly, a series of policy implementation challenges persist. These include 1) stakeholder engagement; 2) skill development and capacity building; and 3) monitoring and evaluation of policy progress. First, individual and corporate property owners need to recognise the benefits of energy efficient buildings as well as supporting schemes, and subnational actions can raise their awareness through further engagement. Second, energy efficiency renovations require skill training and development, in insulation, calculating energy savings, and performance contracts, engaging a broad array of workers across the building value chain. Capacity building in subnational governments is also important. Third, both national and subnational governments need to monitor and evaluate policy progress towards their targets to improve effectiveness of their policies.

The most popular policy implementation measures cited by cities and regions are "Citizen engagement" (76%) and "Pilot and demonstration projects" (57%) (Figure 3.6). In addition, roughly 30% to 40% of cities and regions promote "Locally tailored analysis and planning", "Support to local industry", "Private sector engagement" and "Capacity building in subnational governments". Given how close cities and regions are to citizens and local businesses and how familiar they are with local conditions, these percentages may be considered low.

Cities and regions are also well placed to engage local stakeholders in the business and non-profit sectors. In the business sector, most engage "Utilities" (71%), "Construction" (62%) and "Architecture" (57%) in policy making and implementation associated with energy efficiency in buildings. More than a third of cities and regions engage other types of businesses, including "Equipment manufacturing" (48%), "Local building businesses in general" (48%) and "Real estate" (38%) (Figure 3.7). It is important to engage businesses of whatever size and to engage not only large corporations but also small- and medium-sized enterprises (SMEs). SMEs are key actors, both as major providers of construction and renovation and as energy consumers with limited resources for energy-saving measures.

Figure 3.6. Measures taken by cities and regions to decarbonise buildings

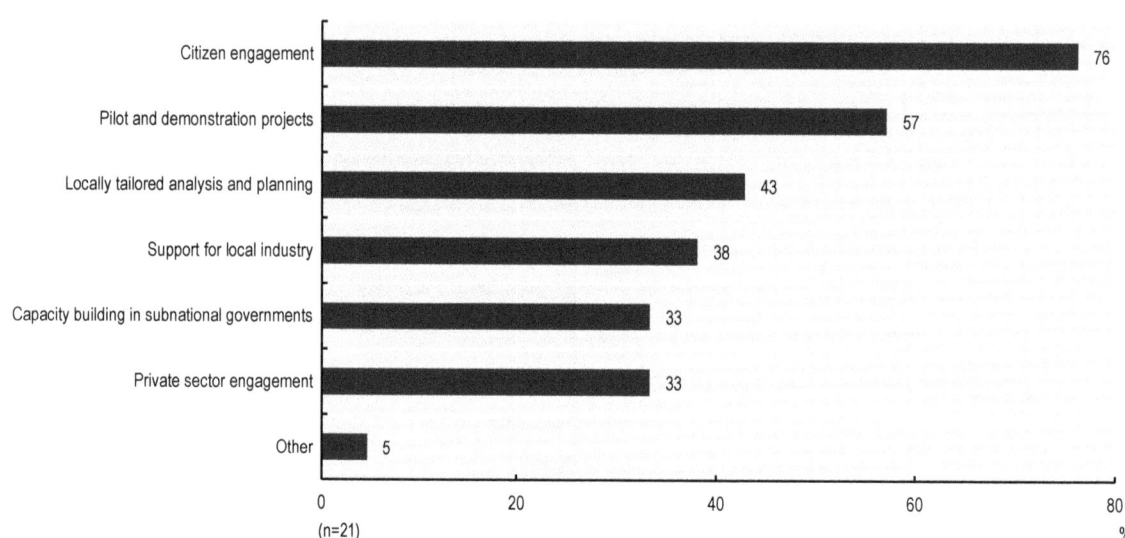

Source: OECD Survey on Decarbonising Buildings in Cities and Regions.

Figure 3.7. Stakeholder engagement (business and utilities sector)

Stakeholder	%
Utilities	71
Construction	62
Architecture	57
Local business in general	48
Equipment manufacturing	48
Real estate	38
Building inspection	33
Energy service company (ESCO)	29
Financial service	24
None	0

(n=21)

Source: OECD Survey on Decarbonising Buildings in Cities and Regions.

As for the non-profit sector, most cities and regions report that they engage "Academia/ research institutes/ universities" (62%), non-profit organisations (57%) and public housing authorities (48%). Few cities and regions engage owners of social housing and landlords' associations, important stakeholders through which they could raise public support and aggregate the need for mass renovations (Figure 3.8). Cities and regions use a variety of ways to engage stakeholders. A large number use "Consultation (meetings, workshops, forums, etc.)" (81%), "Open access to policy documents and data" (48%), and "Co-drafting or partnership (where input has been actively taken into account to shape the policy)" (48%).

Figure 3.8. Stakeholder engagement (non-profit sector)

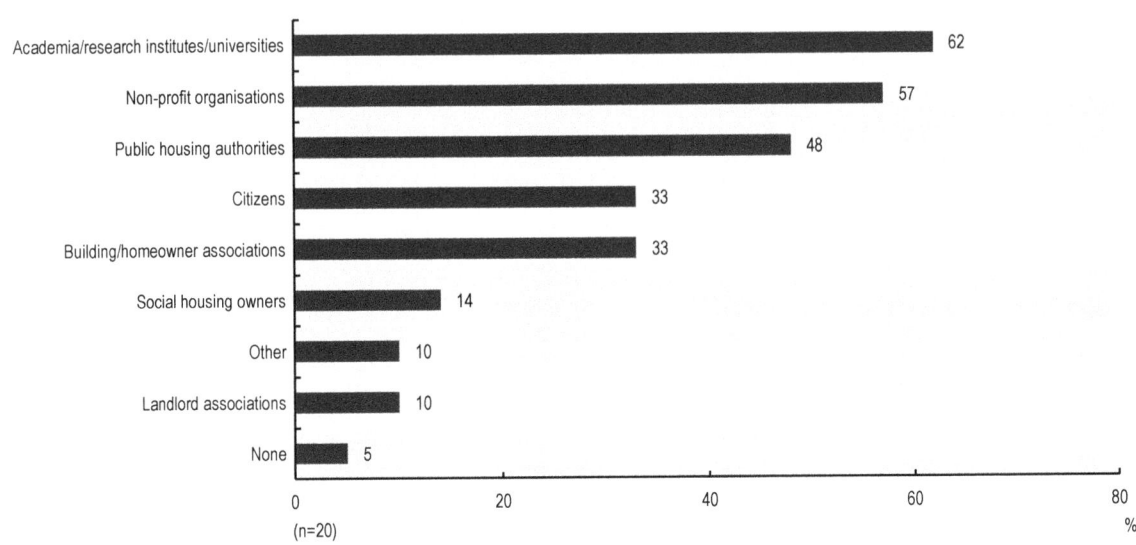

Stakeholder	%
Academia/research institutes/universities	62
Non-profit organisations	57
Public housing authorities	48
Citizens	33
Building/homeowner associations	33
Social housing owners	14
Other	10
Landlord associations	10
None	5

(n=20)

Source: OECD Survey on Decarbonising Buildings in Cities and Regions.

Cities and regions are well placed to engage citizens and local businesses. One popular policy is to set up a "one-stop-shop" for energy efficiency renovation. The Brussels Capital Region in Belgium provides "Sustainable building facilitator" services to citizens for renovation of condominiums, in co-operation with a broad array of stakeholders along the building value chain (EnEffect, n.d.[31]). The City of Tampere in Finland encourages citizens to reduce their energy use by equipping all homes with smart meters and offering free energy advice and a web-based tool for planning energy efficient home renovations (Holm, 2020[32]).

References

APUR (2021), *Vers un service public de la donnée énergétique à Paris*, https://www.apur.org/fr/nos-travaux/vers-un-service-public-donnee-energetique-paris. [30]

BC Housing (2020), *2019 BC Energy Step Code Market Response Study*, https://energystepcode.ca/reports/ (accessed on 23 October 2021). [5]

BC Housing's Research Centre and the Community Energy Association (2019), *2019 BC Energy Step Code Local Government Survey*, https://energystepcode.ca/app/uploads/sites/257/2019/07/FINAL-BC-Energy-Step-Code-Local-Government-Survey-Report-July-2019.pdf. [6]

Brown, D., P. Kivimaa and S. Sorrell (2019), "An energy leap? Business model innovation and intermediation in the 'Energiesprong' retrofit initiative", *Energy Research and Social Science*, Vol. 58, https://doi.org/10.1016/j.erss.2019.101253 (accessed on 23 October 2021). [24]

City of Toronto (n.d.), *Home Energy Loan Program*, https://www.toronto.ca/services-payments/water-environment/environmental-grants-incentives/home-energy-loan-program-help/#:~:text=In%202022%2C%20the%20City%20will%20be%20launching%20an%20enhanced%20Home,the%20enhanced%20program%20launch%20date. (accessed on 25 January 2022). [19]

Clean BC (n.d.), *CleanBC Better Homes Low-Interest Financing Program*, Clean BC Better Homes, https://betterhomesbc.ca/rebates/financing/#:~:text=The%20CleanBC%20Better%20Homes%20Low,system%20to%20a%20heat%20pump. (accessed on 25 January 22). [18]

EC (2020), "Renovation wave: Doubling the renovation rate to cut emissions, boost recovery and reduce energy poverty", European Commission, https://ec.europa.eu/commission/presscorner/detail/en/IP_20_1835 (accessed on 25 January 2022). [17]

EC (2017), "Netherlands, Energiesprong (Energy Leap)", Policy measure fact sheet, European Construction Sector Observatory, https://ec.europa.eu/docsroom/documents/30290/attachments/3/translations/en/renditions/pdf (accessed on 23 October 2021). [26]

EERE (n.d.), *EISA Federal Facility Management and Benchmarking Reporting Requirements*, Office of Energy Efficiency and Renewable Energy, https://www.energy.gov/eere/femp/eisa-federal-facility-management-and-benchmarking-reporting-requirements (accessed on 25 January 2022). [27]

EnEffect (n.d.), *Passive House Regions with Renewable Energies*, https://passreg.eu/download.php?cms=1&file=D_2_1c_Brussels_SM_EN.pdf (accessed on 30 November 2020). [31]

Energiesprong Foundation (n.d.), *Energiesprong*, https://energiesprong.org/ (accessed on 30 November 2020). [22]

Energy Step Code (n.d.), *About the Site and Council*, https://energystepcode.ca/about/. [11]

Energycities (2020), "Innovative energy solutions for subsidized housing: A developers competition for energy efficient timber buildings", https://energy-cities.eu/best-practice/innovative-energy-solutions-for-subsidized-housing/ (accessed on 30 November 2020). [16]

Energycities (2016), "En route for 100% renewable energy in municipal buildings", https://energy-cities.eu/best-practice/en-route-for-100-renewable-energy-in-municipal-buildings/ (accessed on 30 November 2020). [15]

Eurocities (2019), *Cities Leading the Way on Climate Action*, https://eurocities.eu/wp-content/uploads/2020/08/EUROCITIES_cities_climate_action_2019-1.pdf (accessed on 30 November 2020). [3]

Glave, J. and R. Wark (2019), *Lessons from the BC Energy Step Code*, https://www2.gov.bc.ca/assets/gov/farming-natural-resources-and-industry/construction-industry/building-codes-and-standards/reports/bcenergystepcode_lessons_learned_final.pdf (accessed on 23 October 2021). [8]

Government of British Columbia (n.d.), *Energy Step Code*, https://energystepcode.ca/. [7]

Government of France (2020), *Long-term Strategy of France for Mobilising Investment in the Renovation of the National Stock of Residential and Commercial Buildings*, https://ec.europa.eu/energy/sites/default/files/documents/fr_ltrs_2020_en.pdf (accessed on 25 March 2021). [13]

Holm, S. (2020), "Tampere: Engaging housing co-ops and residents in the drive towards carbon neutrality", https://municipalpower.org/articles/tampere-engaging-housing-co-ops-and-residents-in-the-drive-towards-carbon-neutrality/ (accessed on 30 November 2020). [32]

IEA (2021), *Energy Efficiency 2021*, International Energy Agency, https://iea.blob.core.windows.net/assets/9c30109f-38a7-4a0b-b159-47f00d65e5be/EnergyEfficiency2021.pdf (accessed on 10 January 2022). [1]

IEA (2020), *The Netherlands 2020 Energy Policy Review*, International Energy Agency, https://iea.blob.core.windows.net/assets/93f03b36-64a9-4366-9d5f-0261d73d68b3/The_Netherlands_2020_Energy_Policy_Review.pdf (accessed on 28 January 2022). [20]

Knauf Insulation (2021), *Insulation Matters Annual Review 2021*, https://info.knaufinsulation-ts.com/hubfs/Knauf%20Insulation_%20Insulation%20Matters%20Annual%20Review%202021.pdf?utm_campaign=2021%20-%20Sustainability%20report%20-%20FR&utm_medium=email&_hsmi=130114642&_hsenc=p2ANqtz-_tuwubcXWxP0tXnlLqiFmF09KF83KHkrIQqQ (accessed on 28 January 2022). [23]

May, Z. (2020), "Energy Step Code – Building Beyond the Standard", *Webinar – Decarbonising Buildings in Cities and Regions*, https://www.oecd.org/cfe/cities/energy-efficiency-cities.htm. [10]

Ministry of Industry and Trade (2020), *Long-term Renovation Strategy to Support the Renovation of the National Stock of Both Public and Private Residential and Non-residential Buildings*, https://ec.europa.eu/energy/sites/default/files/documents/cz_2020_ltrs_official_translation_en.pdf (accessed on 25 March 2021). [12]

MLIT (2018), *Statistics on Building Stock*, Japanese Ministry of Land, Infrastructure, Transport and Tourism, https://www.mlit.go.jp/report/press/joho04_hh_000785.html (accessed on 25 March, 2021). [14]

New York City Mayor's Office of Sustainability (2019), *The Climate Mobilization Act*, https://www1.nyc.gov/site/sustainability/legislation/climate-mobilization-act-2019.page (accessed on 30 November 2020). [4]

PAW (n.d.), *Factsheet: Programme for Natural Gas-free Districts*. [21]

SF Environment (2021), *San Francisco Climate Action Plan*, https://sfenvironment.org/climateplan (accessed on 25 January 2022). [29]

SFWPS (n.d.), *Municipal Buildings Energy Benchmarking*, San Francisco Water Power Sewer, https://sfpuc.org/about-us/reports/municipal-buildings-energy-benchmarking#:~:text=Power%20BI%20Report&text=In%202011%2C%20the%20San%20Francisco,and%20disclose%20building%20energy%20performance. (accessed on 25 January 2022). [28]

UNEP (2021), *2021 Global Status Report for Buildings and Construction: Towards a Zero-emission, Efficient and Resilient Buildings and Construction Sector*, United Nations Environment Programme, https://globalabc.org/resources/publications/2021-global-status-report-buildings-and-construction (accessed on 26 October 2021). [2]

Vancouver Economic Commission (2019), *Green Buildings Market Forecast: Demand for Building Products, Metro Vancouver 2019–2032*, https://www.vancouvereconomic.com/research/green-buildings-market-research/ (accessed on 23 October 2021). [9]

Visscher, H. (2020), "Innovations for a carbon free Dutch housing stock in 2050", *IOP Conference Series: Earth and Environmental Science*, Vol. 588, http://dx.doi.org/10.1088/1755-1315/588/3/032050 (accessed on 23 October 2021). [25]

4 Key barriers to unlock for scaling up local and regional action

This chapter identifies key barriers facing cities and regions as they scale up their policy actions, based on responses to the OECD Survey on Decarbonising Buildings in Cities and Regions and on the policy dialogue with national government officials in policy seminars. These barriers include insufficient government budget and resources, insufficient incentives to secure the commitment of property owners, the lack of an effective monitoring and evaluation framework and the limited resources of local industries. The chapter also discusses how cities and regions believe the impact of the COVID-19 crisis has affected their ambitions, financing and strategies on decarbonisation of buildings.

Technical solutions and basic policy tools such as building energy codes already exist in some countries to begin the process of decarbonising buildings. In addition, as discussed in the previous chapter, cities and regions have already taken a variety of policy measures, from introducing regulatory tools and frameworks to engaging local actors. However, scaling up the process of decarbonising buildings poses a number of obstacles. Without co-ordinating these policy measures in cities and regions and across levels of government, these measures are unlikely to provide sufficient incentives for property owners. Lack of awareness among citizens and businesses of both the importance of energy efficiency in buildings and its potential benefits has been holding back a rapid transformation of the market. Effective policy monitoring and evaluation will be needed to improve the effectiveness of policy measures and to ensure accountability of public investment. Most of the obstacles pointed out by cities and regions are related to governance gaps, including 1) insufficient budget and resources, 2) a lack of incentives to secure the commitment of property owners, 3) a lack of focus on analysis, planning and monitoring tailored to local circumstances, and 4) a shortage of skilled labour and lack of support for small- and medium-sized enterprises (SMEs). The COVID-19 crisis and accompanying social changes will also have a mixed impact on decarbonising buildings, which requires effective policy implementation and governance.

Despite their potential, cities and regions face major gaps in governance

- **Insufficient government budget and resources**: Of cities and regions that responded to the survey, 76% consider "Insufficient budget and resources" the greatest obstacle to enhancing energy efficiency in buildings, and 48% "Insufficient human resource and technical expertise" (Figure 4.1). These are mainly related to the capacity of local or regional administration and stakeholders to improve energy efficiency in buildings. Financial grants or loans require a significant budget for cities and regions, which limits the expansion of existing local programmes. Further financial support from national or supra-national organisations as a COVID-19 recovery package could help address municipalities' financial needs. The most pressing challenge is to expand the human resources and technical expertise devoted to core functions such as plan making, code enforcement and public building contracting. Without them, it will be difficult to implement new initiatives supported by green recovery packages. Subnational governments need capacity with the relevant technical background to attract, manage and retain external experts to carry out planning, enforcement and undertake such projects.
- **Lack of incentives to secure the commitment of property owners**: In the OECD survey, 30-40% of cities and regions consider "Lack of motivation for property owners" and "Lack of financial incentives for property owners" an obstacle to enhancing energy efficiency in buildings. Unlike public infrastructure owned by the government, private properties cannot be modified without the owners' consent. Upscaling energy efficiency investment in private buildings requires high upfront costs, and is often difficult. Furthermore, split incentives between owners and renters, the difficulty of reaching collective decisions in multifamily housing and competing priorities across property owners (e.g. safety, financial stability) can hold back energy efficiency investment in buildings, even when the benefits are clearly documented. In the absence of appropriate regulations for existing buildings and a clear regulatory push to encourage buy-in from individual property owners, cities and regions will need to devote financial and human resources to engaging and co-ordinating with these owners to invest in energy efficiency. While, at a national level, countries need to develop effective regulatory frameworks for existing buildings, cities and regions can explore additional options through experimentation.
- **Lack of an effective monitoring and evaluation framework**: Although this is not broadly recognised by cities and regions, the clear challenge is to analyse the local building stock and energy performance, develop a long-term plan or strategy and monitor local policy progress. There are a myriad of projects and initiatives on energy efficiency in buildings at local scale. However, it

is not clear how they contribute to the overall targets of cities and regions and whether they are having enough impact. Most indicators used for evaluating policy progress are output-based, which means that cities and regions cannot evaluate their progress relative to overall targets. In addition, cities and regions face more difficulties monitoring and evaluating the progress in private buildings than in public ones. This suggests a need to introduce monitoring and evaluation frameworks such as the use of smart meters or mandatory reporting systems for cities and regions. Considering the rebound effects pointed out by several experts, indicators should monitor the actual energy consumption or carbon emissions from buildings in addition to the improvement in their energy performance.

- **Local businesses' lack of skills, knowledge and financial resources**: Strict energy codes for new buildings, retrofitting and renovation would make buildings more automated, digitised and decarbonised. The workforce to support the design, operation and maintenance of these buildings will need to be trained in the necessary skills. The demand for skilled labour and the supply in local industries is already out of balance. In Canada, for example, the city of Toronto has analysed that the number of competent contractors needs to increase to meet the demand for its ambitious plans for decarbonisation. This labour shortage could increase, especially given that some countries seek to boost the housing supply to increase housing affordability and scale up renovations for decarbonisation. The local employment transformation linked to energy efficiency measures will rely on a specific set of skills. Workers will need to train, reskill, and upskill to meet demand for the energy efficiency market. Building these skills will require concerted efforts from government, industry and key stakeholders (Truitt, Williams and Salzman, 2020[1]). In the survey, when cities and regions were asked about their key priorities for energy efficiency in buildings, 57% of the cities reported that they would need broader engagement of citizens and the private sector and greater awareness raising; and 38% cited greater support for innovative local projects and initiatives (Figure 3.5). SMEs are at the intersection of these two priorities, and local innovative projects and initiatives can attract the private sector. SMEs and entrepreneurs can be a source of innovation and solutions in developing the technology needed for building decarbonisation, and they can also promote energy saving in their offices. Some efforts have been made to support SMEs across countries, and recovery packages play a significant role in sustainable finance and in addressing climate challenges, but SMEs are often neglected in recovery packages (OECD, 2021[2]). In leveraging recovery packages for energy efficiency in buildings, the needs of SMEs should be taken into account.

Figure 4.1. Obstacles faced by cities and regions in decarbonising buildings

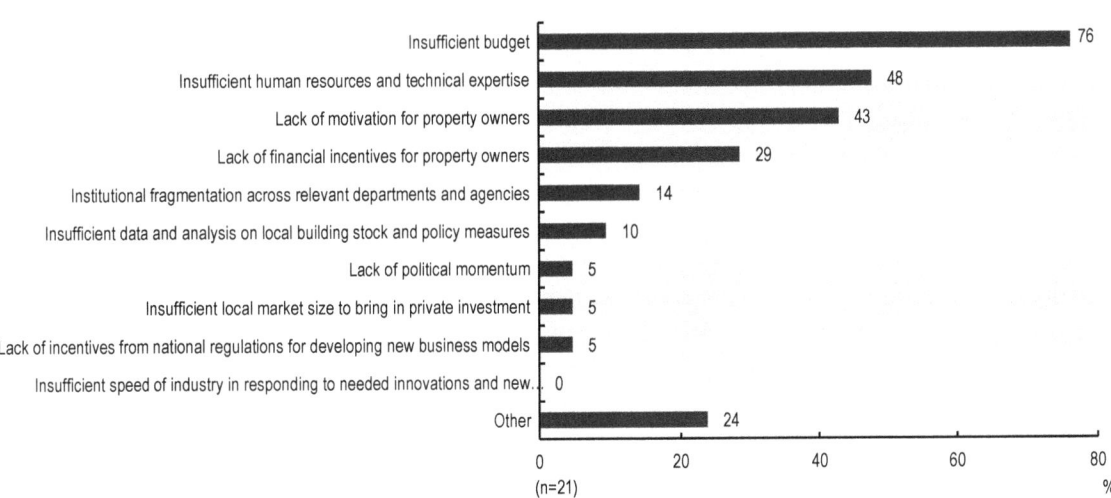

Source: OECD Survey on Decarbonising Buildings in Cities and Regions.

A lack of data makes it hard to ascertain where cities and regions stand in terms of energy efficiency in buildings. Nearly 70% of respondents to the survey strongly agree or agree they have "data/information gaps on monitoring current status and outcomes on energy efficiency in buildings" (e.g. on energy consumption or buildings' energy performance). About half of cities and regions also strongly agree or agree that they face "data/information gaps on assessing policies compared to peer city/region" (e.g. that they lack comparable data on policy framework conditions or energy efficiency outcomes) (Figure 4.2). This clearly shows the need for common monitoring indicators, both within and among countries.

Figure 4.2. Data and information gaps related to building decarbonisation

Statement	Strongly agree	Agree	Disagree	Strongly disagree	Unsure or no opinion	n
Your city/region has data/information gaps on monitoring current status and outcomes on energy efficiency in buildings	11	56	17	11	6	17
Your city/region has data/information gaps on assessing its policies compared to peer city/region	11	39	17	17	17	18
Your city/region has data/information gaps on providing clear rationale for citizens to invest in energy efficiency measures in buildings	11	33	33	17	6	18
Your city/region has data/information gaps on developing clearly defined local plan or strategy related to energy efficiency in buildings	12	24	41	12	12	18

Source: OECD Survey on Decarbonising Buildings in Cities and Regions.

The impact of the COVID-19 crisis has been mixed on decarbonising buildings in cities and regions

The COVID-19 crisis could have both short- and long-term effects on real estate markets, through behavioural changes in working, commuting and shopping patterns. The COVID-19 crisis has had a mixed impact on energy efficiency improvements in buildings. Negative impacts cited by cities and regions include "Less demand for private energy efficiency investment in buildings due to economic downturn" (39%) and "Less public expenditure for energy efficiency in buildings due to rising public deficit" (28%), while positive effects include "Greater demand for home retrofits or renovations as a place to telework" (28%) and "Greater needs for energy efficiency retrofits or renovations for low-income households to ensure energy affordability" (28%). Only 11% reported a "Slowdown due to declining construction activity" and 6% reported "Greater public expenditure for energy efficiency in buildings from COVID-19 recovery packages", which is low, considering the extensive plans for investment in national recovery packages (Figure 4.3). One explanation could be that it is still unclear how these investments and funding will be allocated. Considering the amount of funding needed to renovate urban buildings, the recovery packages need to provide clear guidance on how these resources will be distributed and allocate a significant amount to subnational governments. Some cities and regions included energy efficiency measures in buildings in their COVID-19 recovery plans or strategies, including providing financial incentives for construction and energy efficient renovations of private housing and public buildings. In the long run, cities and regions need to identify major impacts of the COVID-19 crisis on building decarbonisation and adjust their policies to changing policy environments.

Figure 4.3. Cities' and regions' perception of the impact of COVID-19 on decarbonisation of buildings

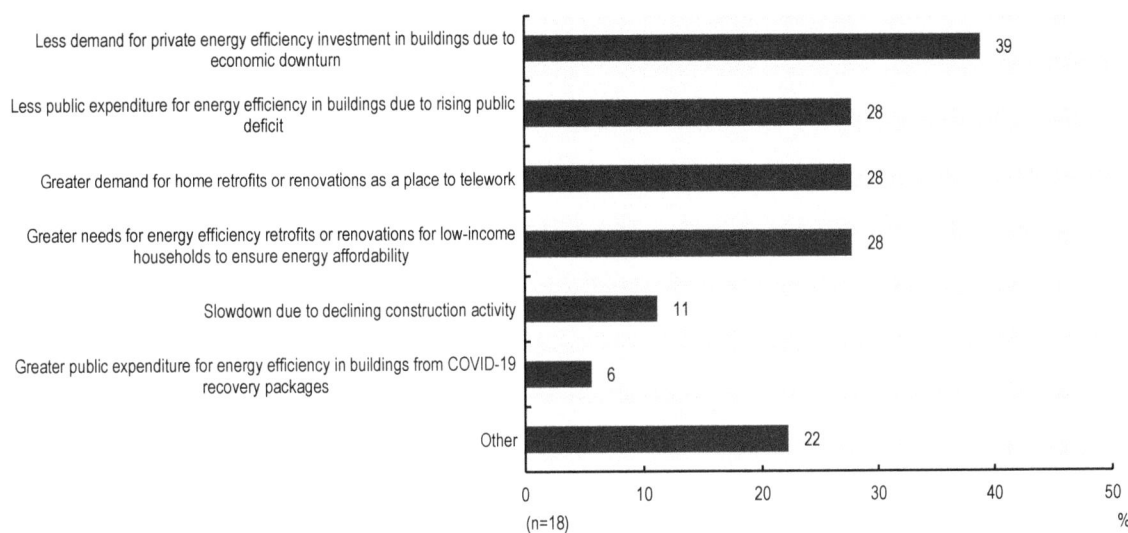

Source: OECD Survey on Decarbonising Buildings in Cities and Regions.

References

OECD (2021), "No net zero without SMEs: Exploring the key issues for greening SMEs and green entrepreneurship", *OECD SME and Entrepreneurship Papers*, No. 30, OECD Publishing, Paris, https://dx.doi.org/10.1787/bab63915-en. [2]

Truitt, S., J. Williams and M. Salzman (2020), *Building the Efficiency Workforce: Preprint*, National Renewable Energy Laboratory, https://www.nrel.gov/docs/fy20osti/75497.pdf (accessed on 26 January 2022). [1]

5 A Checklist for Public Action to scale up building decarbonisation

This chapter first discusses the vital role of national governments in promoting a whole-of-government and multilevel governance approach to decarbonising buildings and creating the enabling environments for subnational actors to unlock their potential. Then, it proposes a checklist for both national and subnational governments to scale up building decarbonisation in cities and regions. The checklist aims to support the key roles of subnational governments in planning, leadership and engagement to promote building decarbonisation, and provides recommendations for national governments to set a common policy framework across cities and regions. It also provides relevant policy examples from leading cities, regions and countries.

The key role of national governments in setting the enabling environment

National governments can play a vital role in promoting a whole-of-government and multilevel governance approach to decarbonising buildings. They also create the enabling environments for subnational actors to unlock their potential and scale up action in this field. This includes factoring local considerations into national policies, encouraging local innovation and supporting subnational governments in building capacity. In addition, national governments can help develop a subnational database and indicators, to allow subnational governments to assess progress in reaching their own targets, and to compare how they are doing in comparison with peer cities and regions domestically and globally.

Energy efficiency in buildings involves multiple policy areas, such as housing and building policy, energy policy and environmental policy. Horizontal and vertical policy alignment and co-ordination is essential to provide a coherent long-term vision and support to cities and regions. Three ministries in Japan, the Ministry of Land, Infrastructure, Transport and Tourism, the Ministry of Economy, Trade and Industry and the Ministry of the Environment, have developed a roadmap on policies to promote decarbonisation in housing and buildings, from energy efficiency, renewable energy use and carbon storage, spelling out the roles of relevant ministries (MLIT, 2021[1]). Before discussing the national governments' role, it is important to map out the line or sectoral ministries responsible for energy efficiency in buildings. As reported in the OECD survey, these competences lie mostly in the "Ministry of Energy or equivalent" (41%), "Ministry of the Environment or equivalent" (35%), "Ministry of Housing and Urban Development or equivalent" (24%) or in some cases, more than two ministries (29%).

Without an effective and appropriate national regulatory framework for existing buildings, cities and regions may not have the resources or authority to keep up with the targets called for in national plans or strategies. About a third of cities and regions that responded to the survey reported challenges in vertical co-ordination on energy efficiency in buildings across subnational and national governments in their countries. National policy can sometimes diverge from its implementation in a local context, both in terms of levels of ambition and the priorities of policy measures to be taken.

As for the support they received from national governments, 74% of the cities and regions surveyed considered it to be inadequate (Figure 5.1). Asked to specify the type of support they needed, 95% cited "Financial support to advanced projects" and 74% "Awareness raising in general public". Most cities and regions have started their own projects or initiatives and are now facing budget constraints and a lack of motivation among property owners as they try to expand these programmes. "Removing barriers in national regulations that inhibit innovative local actions" and "Capacity building support" is also cited as a priority for 58% of respondents (Figure 5.2). In response to these challenges, national governments could promote dialogue with subnational governments and actors, and identify and adjust regulations that prevent new solutions at the local level. National governments can also develop databases to build capacity and provide information that cities and regions can use to conduct localised analysis and planning. This can also contribute to raising awareness, providing more convincing evidence of the benefits of energy efficiency investment in buildings. The survey also asked how much cities and regions utilise funding from multilateral development banks, supranational or other international donors. While European cities and regions tend to make moderate use of supranational or international donors, most cities and regions do not receive funding from international sources.

Figure 5.1. Share of cities and regions that receive enough support from national governments

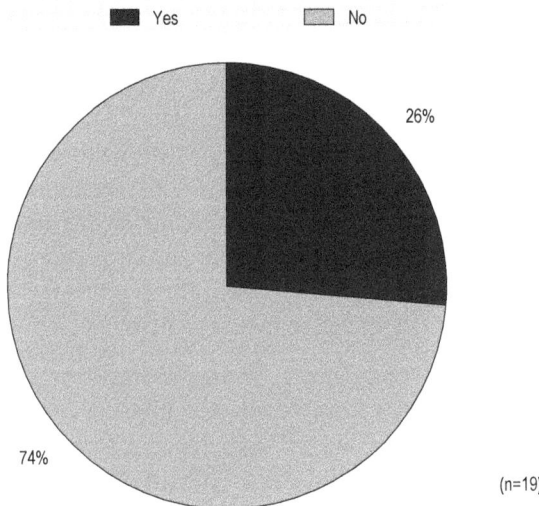

Source: OECD Survey on Decarbonising Buildings in Cities and Regions.

Figure 5.2. Type of national government support cities and regions require

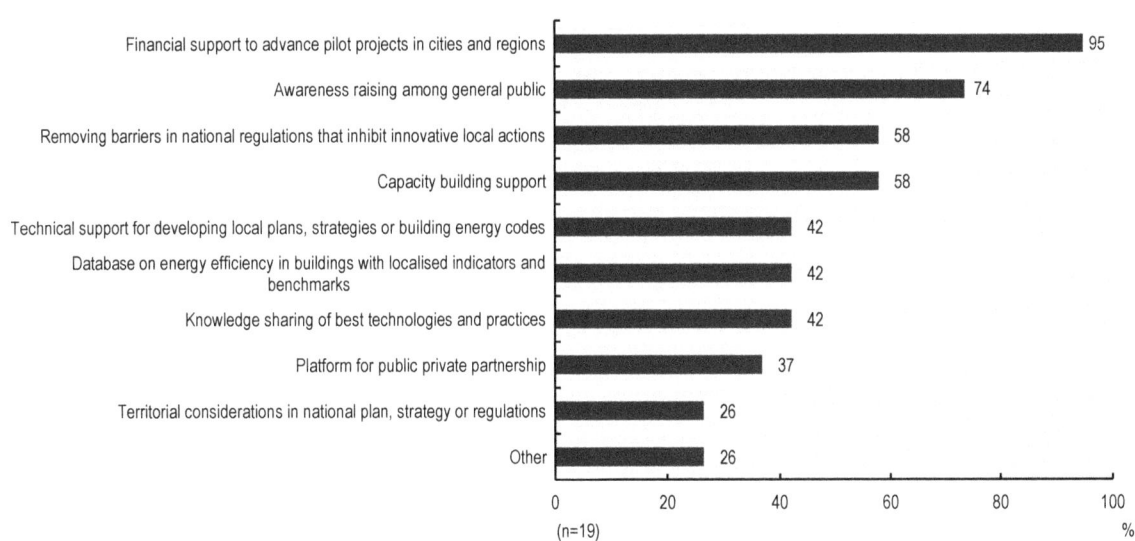

Source: OECD Survey on Decarbonising Buildings in Cities and Regions.

A Checklist for Public Action to decarbonise buildings in cities and regions

Cities and regions have a holistic role to play, sharing responsibility with national governments and the private sector in the decarbonisation of buildings. National governments play a vital role in setting the basic framework that enables stakeholders in both private and public sectors to decarbonise buildings, leveraging their legislative authority and access to the best available technical and financial resources in a country. Their role includes developing common policy tools and frameworks in cities and regions; enhancing multilevel policy co-ordination; and providing guidance and support to cities and regions. This provides indispensable framework conditions for cities and regions to promote building decarbonisation.

As noted in Chapter 3, cities and regions can play a major role in four policy areas: regulations; financing; planning and co-ordination; and engagement of local actors. These policy measures do not work on their own and need to be closely co-ordinated to produce the intended goals and synergies. A single policy, such as mandatory building energy codes or a subsidy for energy efficiency renovations, cannot create enough momentum for the transition to low-carbon building stock. The policy measures need to be mutually intertwined and strengthen each other, if carefully designed. Cities and regions thus need to develop a comprehensive policy package and consider how their policy measures can create synergy. They can use public building projects to raise public awareness, engage local businesses and make a business case for private financing. Engaging construction and relevant industries in the planning process may help introduce ambitious but appropriate regulations that local industries can actively prepare for. Meanwhile, providing a long-term vision, in particular of public investment, may offer a basis for a more stable market with a view to retaining and expanding skilled labour in the relevant sectors.

Cities and regions need to identify key challenges, as well as local resources available, and create locally tailored strategies to address bottlenecks in effective and efficient ways, making the best use of limited local resources. As noted in Chapter 4, key barriers to upscaling subnational policy actions include: insufficient budget and resources; lack of incentives to secure the commitment of property owners; lack of an effective monitoring and evaluation framework; and a shortage of skilled labour and insufficient support for small- and medium-sized enterprises (SMEs). They can engage a variety of stakeholders, including not only citizens and local businesses but housing and building owners. They can also include construction and supporting industries to promote the transition to the low-carbon building stock as a whole. Subnational governments need to chart a clear vision, to lead by example and to design and apply appropriate governance mechanisms.

The OECD Checklist for Public Action builds on key findings from the report and the underlying survey, insights from policy dialogues with key stakeholders, and a stock-taking of existing guidance to decarbonise buildings for national government, which has paved the way for complementary place-based recommendations. It provides guidance for cities and regions to accelerate and manage the transition to a low-carbon building society in cities and regions. It also offers national governments assistance in setting up a common framework that creates the enabling environments in cities and regions. It builds on three national policy recommendations; and nine subnational policy recommendations, grouped into three pillars that correspond to the key roles of cities and regions: 1) plan; 2) lead; and 3) engage (Figure 5.3):

- **Plan**: Cities and regions can chart a way forward in the transition to low-carbon building stock by: creating a common vision for a broad array of stakeholders; devising effective local regulatory frameworks for building decarbonisation and co-ordinating them with national policy; and introducing an effective scheme for monitoring and evaluating policy progress.
- **Lead**: Cities and regions can lead by example to scale up building decarbonisation by: leveraging public building procurement for broader objectives; promoting pilot projects and innovative business models; and incentivising and co-ordinating renovation needs to create economies of scale.
- **Engage**: Cities and regions can enlist a broad array of stakeholders, citizens and local businesses to take action, by: raising awareness among citizens and local businesses; providing support for low-income households and SMEs; and building capacity in subnational governments and local industries.

| 69

Figure 5.3. A Checklist for Public Action to Decarbonise Buildings in Cities and Regions

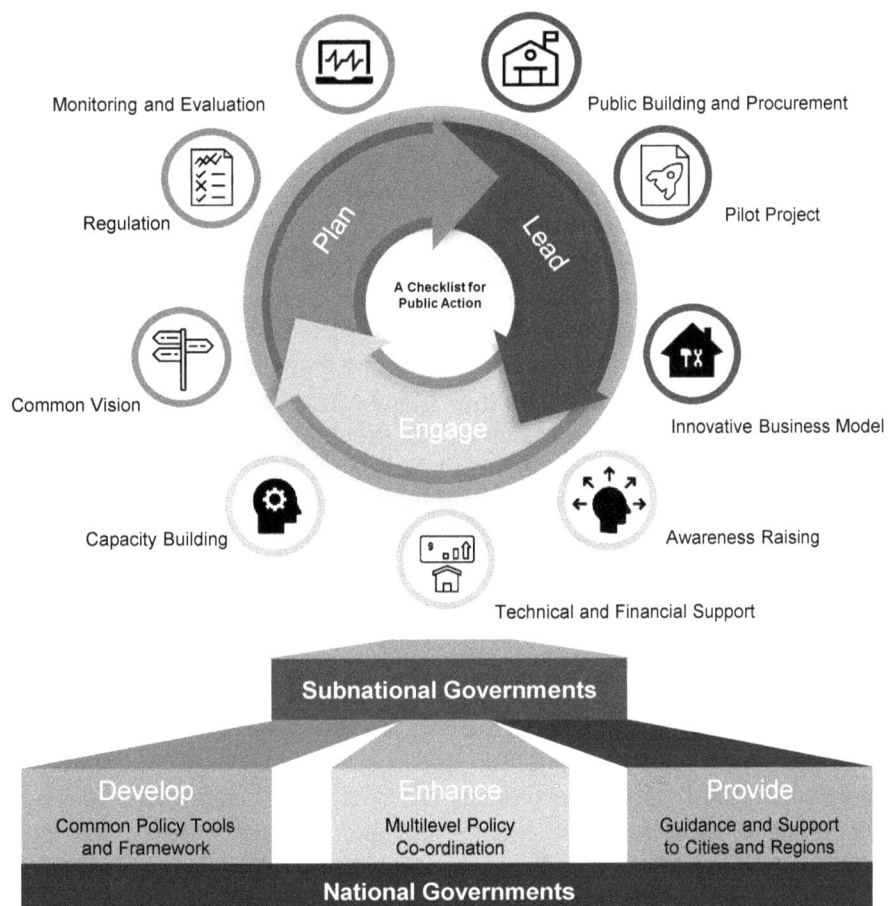

National governments can provide a common framework across cities and regions

Develop common policy tools and framework across cities and regions

Some policy levers, in particular the regulatory framework, rely principally on national governments. Although cities and regions are in charge of developing their own building codes or introducing restrictions through ordinances in some countries, basic regulations need to be designed by national governments, since construction activities span different subnational jurisdictions. From a business perspective, full compliance with a variety of building regulations in cities and regions is a major investment. From a public perspective, a small city or a remote region does not have the power to influence the private market. Furthermore, developing new regulations to address challenges that may arise, such as reducing embodied carbon, calls for a significant amount of technical resources that a single city or region cannot take on alone. National governments should thus provide, at a minimum, the basic regulatory framework and common measurement indicators reflecting the latest scientific and technical knowledge. France, for example, has introduced regulations for new construction that require a life-cycle carbon assessment, including the carbon emissions generated during both the construction and the demolition of buildings (Ministry of the Ecological Transition, 2021[2]). In Finland in 2017, the Ministry of the Environment published a roadmap for decarbonised construction intended to be adopted by the mid-2020s for the life-cycle carbon footprint of buildings. The first assessment method in construction projects was introduced in the autumn of 2019, and Finland is now moving towards legislative adoption of life-cycle assessment in its construction industry (EC, 2020[3]).

Another important role of national governments is to ensure that energy prices reflect the real social and environmental costs, through carbon pricing or other mechanisms. Setting the right price incentives is important, because the low prices of fossil fuels compared to clean energy sources deter both individuals and businesses from investing in energy efficiency and clean energy in buildings. In 2021, Germany launched carbon-pricing schemes in the form of national Emissions Trading System (ETS) for heating and transport fuels (International Carbon Action Partnership, 2021[4]). The national government also needs to develop a common framework for measuring and certifying buildings' energy performance in cities and regions. For example, all European Union (EU) member countries promote energy performance certification schemes at the national level based on the Energy Performance of Buildings Directive (EPBD) (BPIE, 2014[5]; EC, n.d.[6]). This is particularly relevant, as more than half of the cities and regions surveyed report data gaps that make it difficult to compare their policy conditions and outcomes with peer cities and regions. National governments can disclose subnational breakdowns of national statistical data so that cities and regions can compare not only energy and carbon outcomes, but also relevant factors policy makers must consider, such as housing affordability and energy poverty. In addition, they can facilitate the use of common measurement indicators among cities and regions to evaluate regional and local conditions.

Most cities and regions surveyed (74%) also expect support from national governments in raising public awareness of the issue. This is also a policy area national governments can promote effectively, by collecting information on the benefits of building decarbonisation from pilot funding programmes and platforms for multilevel dialogues, and disclosing the data for cities, regions and private organisations. This can help make the case for further investment in decarbonising buildings. In Japan, for example, the national government supported experimental projects to collect health-related data before and after energy efficiency retrofits, enlisting experts in both architecture and medical science, and then subsequently sharing the evidence on health benefits from those retrofits with the relevant constituencies (MLIT, 2019[7]).

Enhance multilevel policy co-ordination

There are substantial needs at local scale for national support on funding and technical expertise. However, energy efficiency policies in buildings usually involve several ministries and agencies at the national level. If cities and regions are to acquire the necessary sustained support from national governments, co-ordination among relevant ministries and agencies and across levels of government is needed. In addition, policy coherence across levels of government is required, to provide the right incentives for building owners and investors. One of the first steps is to create a multilevel platform to share subnational policy practices and developments in national policy, to discuss issues around policy implementation and to align policies related to building decarbonisation. Updated national policy developments are beneficial for cities and regions to draw additional resources, while the information on the obstacles at local scale help national governments identify the potential need for policy reform at the national level.

National authorities can also facilitate plans and strategies at the subnational level, and incorporate policy reform and support for cities and regions in national plans and strategies. The government of the Netherlands worked with more than 100 parties to reach the Dutch Climate Agreement in 2019, clarifying the roles and responsibilities of each level of government. Municipalities were designated as responsible for planning and co-ordination, regions for spatial planning and regional co-operation, and the national government for financial support to local authorities, information and knowledge sharing and regulation (Government of the Netherlands, 2019[8]).

Provide guidance and support for cities and regions

Nearly all the cities surveyed expect national governments to provide financial resources for advanced projects. A lack of budgetary resources is the greatest obstacle to enhancing energy efficiency in buildings that cities and regions face, together with the lack of financial incentives for property owners. To explore effective ways to decarbonise buildings and replicate successful cases on a broader scale, national governments could consider financial support to advanced pilot projects and promote the lessons of these pilot cases. In the Dutch case mentioned above, the national government promotes a Programme for Natural-gas-free neighbourhoods from 2018 to 2028 that provides an average of EUR 4 million in funding for district-based projects. These involve a variety of techniques, financial schemes and approaches to engage residents and to pass on the experiences learned from pilot projects (IEA, 2020[9]). National governments can also widely share cost-effective technologies and policy solutions as well as green financing schemes, to encourage efficient subnational public investment. Green recovery packages are another possible funding source for subnational projects. SME greening measures can also broaden the base of the decarbonisation of buildings (OECD, 2021[10]).

Cities and regions also noted that a lack of human resources and technical expertise is a major obstacle to building decarbonisation. In particular, a lack of technical expertise and human resources in core functions such as plan making, code enforcement and public building contracting may prevent smooth and effective policy implementation, even if green recovery packages can help to address some subnational financial needs. National governments can monitor and identify pressing human resources and capacity needs in dialogue with cities and regions and provide technical support and capacity-building opportunities for local authorities, to enhance their implementation capacity. Both Ireland and the United Kingdom (UK) have provided guidance documents on ESCOs (energy service companies) contracting in public building procurement, so that public authorities know how to promote energy efficiency measures in public buildings with an ESCO business model (Boza-Kiss, Bertoldi and Economidou, 2014[11]). In Finland, the national government has set up a competence centre for green public procurement, which supports municipalities on low-carbon construction projects (Ministry of Economic Affaris and Employment of Finland, n.d.[12]).

The lack of resources in local industries is a key obstacle for cities and regions. Many countries report that labour shortages must be addressed in scaling up green investment. Cities and regions can collaborate with local industries, identify local skills needs and provide training for the local workforce, but national governments can also help expand the skilled labour base, including in remote communities, by offering training programmes in co-operation with nationwide business associations and expert organisations. Natural Resources Canada, for example, collaborates with training organisations on online training for a new workforce in the energy efficiency sector and an energy advisor recruitment training campaign to support retrofitting, while focusing on increasing equity and representation of Indigenous communities (Natural Resources Canada, 2020[13]). In line with this effort, Canada launched the Canada Greener Homes Grant initiative in May 2021 to provide up to CAD 5 000 for homeowners to renovate their homes. As of January 2022, more than 180 000 home owners applied for this initiative, which called for even more demand for energy advisors. In this initiative, Natural Resources Canada creates a nationwide certification framework for energy advisors, who evaluate both pre-retrofit and post-retrofit energy performance of homes, informs on the courses provided by training organisations, and provides financial support to certain provinces to increase skilled labour. It promised CAD 903 000 investment for the province of Manitoba, which includes training up to an additional 2 000 energy advisors and recruiting 90 energy advisors (Natural Resources Canada, 2022[14]). Meanwhile, promoting new technologies and cost-efficient production methods for energy efficiency renovations can also help cities and regions tackle building decarbonisation with a limited amount of skilled labour, in cost-effective ways.

Subnational governments can help realise building decarbonisation in cities and regions

Plan and chart a way forward

Create a common vision for a broad array of stakeholders

Although most cities and regions (86%) have their own plans and strategies for energy efficiency in buildings, some do not. Decarbonisation of buildings requires local policy considerations, such as climatic conditions, building stock characteristics, housing affordability, energy poverty, preparedness of local industries and district-scale energy infrastructure. Cities and regions need to factor in these local elements and provide a long-term, common vision for a broad array of key stakeholders, including property owners (e.g. homeowners, landlords, housing authorities, large firms with own buildings, rental office owners, real estate firms) and service providers (e.g. architects, construction firms, energy companies, energy advisors, financial institutions, manufacturers of building materials and equipment). To accelerate decarbonisation of the overall building stock, the plans and strategies need to include long-term goals and targets, roles and responsibilities of key stakeholders, and a roadmap towards the goals with concrete interim steps. Buildings are owned by a variety of entities, including private households and SMEs, which is quite different from infrastructure such as roads and bridges, which are owned mainly by public authorities. The plans and strategies need to be supported by a comprehensive set of policy packages with not only policy measures for public buildings but a mix of regulations and incentives for the whole building stock. The city of Vancouver has developed a Zero Emissions Building Plan that lays out specific strategies for different types of buildings with a comprehensive set of regulations and incentives, including greenhouse gas intensity limits, tax reduction, expedited permitting and partial relaxation of zoning regulations (City of Vancouver, 2016[15]).

Devise effective regulatory frameworks for building decarbonisation

- **Introduce or strengthen the enforcement of building energy codes**: Building energy codes have not been established in most cities and regions across the globe. When they have, only 70% are mandatory, and too few require zero-energy targets. Considering the extremely low rate of new construction, the first step for cities and regions is to put in place mandatory building energy codes for new construction, where such codes are not set up, and strengthen code enforcement at the design and construction stages. Without effective code enforcement in both design and construction, strict building energy codes alone cannot ensure the energy performance of buildings.
- **Develop a long-term vision for stricter regulations**: Large cities in high-income countries with greater human and financial resources should apply strict standards to new buildings (e.g. zero energy building level). In applying ambitious new standards, cities and regions should develop a long-term vision and ensure clarity for the construction and its supporting industries to prepare for stricter regulations, while paying attention to ensuring housing affordability, especially for low- and middle-income households. The Province of British Columbia has engaged key industry stakeholders and successfully introduced net-zero energy standards, by developing a shared long-term roadmap and interim targets, so that industries can prepare for its ambitious level of requirements (Box 3.1). For small municipalities that are not big enough to influence the private market, it is suggested that cities as a group or a region co-ordinate to create common zero-energy building standards.
- **Explore effective regulations for existing buildings**: While very few cities and regions seem to apply building energy codes to all buildings, some have started to introduce other types of regulatory measures for existing buildings, including mandatory certification of building energy performance, mandatory reporting of energy consumption or carbon emissions and mandatory

emissions caps. Cities should further explore effective regulations for existing buildings, starting from public housing and buildings as well as large commercial buildings. The policy options that cities and regions can explore include requiring a certain level of energy efficiency for existing buildings by a certain deadline, based on energy performance certification, restricting the renting and sale of buildings below a certain energy performance and introducing mandatory energy reporting systems. In particular, mandatory energy reporting can help create the baseline on energy consumption for similar types of buildings against which property managers can compare their own energy consumption and examine energy efficiency measures. This will also lay the groundwork for more stringent regulations such as carbon emissions caps for existing buildings. The city of San Francisco has introduced an energy benchmarking ordinance requiring annual benchmarking and disclosure of energy performance of commercial buildings and multifamily housing. It resulted in a 10% reduction of energy use in four years (SFWPS, n.d.[16]). Cities and regions also need to consider offering financial support to alleviate the impact of regulations, particularly to vulnerable households and SMEs.

Introduce effective monitoring and evaluation for policy outcomes

- **Assess local policy environments using available local data**: As noted in Chapter 2, policy environments differ across cities and regions depending on climatic conditions, the characteristics of building stock (e.g. size, type, tenure, age, energy performance), construction activities (e.g. the rate of new construction and renovation), energy and carbon emissions outcomes, and socio-economic conditions (e.g. housing affordability, energy poverty). However, these data are not always available at subnational level for policy making and comparable across cities and regions. Cities and regions need to compile the local data and indicators available to assess local policy environments and trends and expand datasets, by obtaining subnational breakdown of national data and exploring local data collection on key indicators.
- **Develop outcome-based indicators to track the outcomes of policy against subnational targets**: Monitoring and evaluation is needed to explore effective policy measures, and to identify areas where more public support is needed. Current subnational practices typically have ambitious long-term targets and short-term individual programme outputs (e.g. the number of renovated housing units in a subsidy programme, or the energy performance of buildings in a newly developed low-carbon district). To evaluate their policy outcomes against their targets in energy or carbon emissions reduction, cities and regions need to know how much the energy performance of buildings has improved and how much energy consumption or carbon emissions have been reduced as a result of the improvements, not only for buildings involved in subnational programmes, but also for the overall building stock. Tracking the energy performance and energy consumption of private buildings is challenging without comprehensive regulations for systematically collecting such data. Cities and regions need first to track energy performance and energy consumption in buildings with the local data available. Monitoring schemes, such as mandatory energy performance certification at the point of sale or rent or mandatory energy reporting systems, can help evaluate progress in private properties.

Lead by example

Leverage public buildings and procurement for broader objectives

- **Apply stricter energy efficiency requirements to public buildings**: Subnational governments own a large number of public buildings, including government offices, public schools and public housing. Given the difficulty of motivating individual property owners, prioritising energy efficiency improvements in public properties can jump-start progress in building decarbonisation. Given limited public budgets, the priority should be public buildings. Most cities and regions (95%) that responded to the OECD survey already promote energy efficiency measures for public buildings. Cities and regions should first consider applying higher levels of energy efficiency requirements, such as zero-energy buildings, to their public buildings.

- **Use public building projects to promote broader energy efficiency investment**: Cities and regions can use public building projects (e.g. energy efficiency renovations, installing smart meters, new construction) as an opportunity to explore and test new technology (e.g. digitalised energy management, new building materials) and business models (e.g. ESCOs) and to give local businesses a chance to test and improve the knowledge and skills acquired in real projects. Energy savings and health benefits should be monitored before and after renovation, to make the business case for private investment and to incentivise the public. Cities and regions can work with private companies, as in the *Energiesprong* programme (Box 3.2) and Knauf Energy Solutions in Belgium (Knauf Insulation, 2021[17]).
- **Adjust public building procurement processes to consider the benefits over the building life cycle**: Public building procurement processes need to be adjusted so cities and regions can select contractors based on the value created over a building's life cycle. The criteria used in public procurement often focus on the costs upfront, which discourages the introduction of innovative technologies and business models.

Promote pilot projects

- **Promote pilot projects**: More than half of the cities and regions surveyed (57%) promote pilot and demonstration projects. These are needed to experiment with new technologies and solutions, to examine possible options and results for building decarbonisation, to showcase the benefits to a wider audience and to raise public awareness of building decarbonisation. Cities and regions can identify development opportunities in the context of urban regeneration and actively co-ordinate pilot projects such as low-carbon district developments or mass renovation programmes. As in the case of public building projects, cities and regions can negotiate with developers or building owners to track energy outcomes and produce compelling evidence.
- **Leverage green finance to boost energy efficiency investment in buildings**: Limited funds are the greatest obstacle to enhancing energy efficiency in buildings faced by cities and regions, together with the lack of financial incentives for property owners. Cities and regions should take advantage of green finance to fill the financing gap in subnational budgets to fund building decarbonisation programmes. The Metropole of Lille in France, for example, included energy efficient renovation investment in its EUR 66 million recovery plan (OECD, 2020[18]) Multilateral development banks such as the European Investment Bank and the Council of Europe Development Bank offer cities and regions loans to invest in energy renovations (EIB, 2021[19]). Cities and regions can also consider issuing green bonds for building renovations, as in the United States (U.S. Department of Energy, n.d.[20])

Encourage innovative business models

To secure social and political buy-in for energy efficiency measures among key stakeholders, they must be convenient, reasonable and meaningful. Some businesses try to realise this by introducing innovative business models, such as financing upfront costs by future energy savings (e.g. ESCO), reducing the cost and time of energy efficiency renovations by using prefabricated walls and roofs, providing clear evidence of the energy-saving benefits by introducing a real-time energy-tracking system, and developing high-performance building materials. Cities and regions should consider encouraging and promoting such innovative business models, using public building procurement and pilot projects and creating a platform for property owners and businesses, including entrepreneurs and SMEs. To take advantage of economies of scale and cut costs, some renovations should be bundled. Energy efficiency renovations also reduce district energy needs, where district heating is installed. Beyond public buildings, cities and regions can consider facilitating renovations at a district or neighbourhood level, invite private investment and reduce production costs. Dutch municipalities, for example, are responsible for planning and co-ordinating the transition to natural-gas-free neighbourhoods, with financial support from the national government (PAW, n.d.[21]).

Engage all stakeholders

Raise awareness among citizens and local businesses

Nearly 60% of the cities and regions surveyed consider broader engagement of citizens and the private sector and greater awareness raising as among their key priorities. They are close to citizens and local businesses and well-placed to raise awareness among them. They can also promote advisory services for general households. The Brussels Capital Region in Belgium provides citizens with technical assistance services on renovating condominiums and co-operating with the private sector (Cicmanova, Eisermann and Maraquin, 2020[22]). Another option available is to compile evidence on the status and benefits of building decarbonisation from public buildings, pilot projects and other resources and inform citizens about them. Paris, for example, provides a digital map with basic building data such as area, construction periods and energy performance, to facilitate building renovations (APUR, 2021[23]).

Provide technical and financial support for low-income households and SMEs

- **Offer technical and financial support to low-income households**: Energy poverty is a pressing issue in many countries. In addition, 89% of cities and regions surveyed view reduced energy bills for low-income households as a primary benefit of energy efficiency in buildings. Upfront investment in energy efficiency measures may increase housing costs for these low-income families, however. Due to historically poor investment in the built environment of low-income neighbourhoods, they are especially susceptible to heat island effects. Energy efficiency renovations will also improve housing conditions and residents' health and well-being. Cities and regions need to incentivise technical and financial support for improving the energy efficiency of low-income housing, as does British Columbia, which provides free energy-saving equipment installation for low-income households (CleanBC, 2022[24]).
- **Provide technical and financial support to SMEs**: Governments often provide broad technical and financial support to households in energy efficiency measures. Although SMEs account for 30% to 60% of energy consumption in the business sector and have limited technical and financial resources, they are not usually targeted for such greening measures. Cities and regions can provide technical assistance on energy management, including small adjustment on equipment and appliance management as well as financing (e.g. loans and loan guarantees) to energy efficiency renovations by building owners that rent space for SMEs. Italy's Emilia Romagna region, for example, offers SMEs energy diagnosis support (Emilia Romagna STARTUP, n.d.[25]).

Build capacity in subnational governments and local industry

- **Promote capacity building in subnational governments**: Cities and regions cited insufficient human resources and technical expertise as a major obstacle to building decarbonisation. Lack of technical expertise and human resources for such core functions as plan making, code enforcement and public building contracting can hold back policy implementation. Cities and regions should take advantage of local resources such as universities and research institutes and collaborate with local businesses to address the lack of technical expertise. They can also optimise the available opportunities provided by national authorities and expert associations.

- **Facilitate skills development of the local workforce**: Chapter 4 identified the lack of resources in local industries as a key obstacle faced by cities and regions. Many countries note that labour shortages must be addressed to scale up green investment. Cities and regions can work with local industries, identify local skills needs and provide training for the local workforce. They can also collaborate with private companies and entrepreneurs to test cost-efficient methods of energy efficiency renovations (e.g. prefabricated walls and roofs that reduce costs and construction time) to address shortages of skilled labour.

References

APUR (2021), *Vers un service public de la donnée énergétique à Paris*, https://www.apur.org/fr/nos-travaux/vers-un-service-public-donnee-energetique-paris. [23]

Boza-Kiss, B., P. Bertoldi and M. Economidou (2014), *Energy Service Companies in the EU: Status review and recommendations for further market development with a focus on Energy Performance Contracting*, Publications Office of the European Union, http://dx.doi.org/10.2760/12258. [11]

BPIE (2014), *Energy Performance Certificates across the EU*, https://www.bpie.eu/wp-content/uploads/2015/10/Energy-Performance-Certificates-EPC-across-the-EU.-A-mapping-of-national-approaches-2014.pdf. [5]

Cicmanova, J., M. Eisermann and T. Maraquin (2020), *How to Set Up a One-stop Shop for Integrated Home Energy Renovation? A Step-by-step Guide for Local Authorities and Other Actors*, https://energy-cities.eu/wp-content/uploads/2020/07/INNOVATE_guide_final.pdf. [22]

City of Vancouver (2016), *Zero Emissions Buildings Plan*, https://vancouver.ca/files/cov/zero-emissions-building-plan.pdf. [15]

CleanBC (2022), *Energy Conservation Assistance Program*, CleanBC Better Homes, https://betterhomesbc.ca/rebates/free-upgrades-bc-hydro-fortisbc-energy-conservation-assistance-program/ (accessed on 28 January 2022). [24]

EC (2020), *Long-term Renovation Strategy 2020-2050 Finland*, European Commission, https://ec.europa.eu/energy/sites/ener/files/documents/fi_2020_ltrs_en.pdf. [3]

EC (n.d.), *Energy Performance Certificates*, European Commission, https://ec.europa.eu/energy/eu-buildings-factsheets-topics-tree/energy-performance-certificates_en. [6]

EIB (2021), *Energy Efficiency Home Renovation - Green Loan*, European Investment Bank, https://www.eib.org/fr/projects/pipelines/all/20210386. [19]

Emilia Romagna STARTUP (n.d.), *Smart City and Building*, https://www.emiliaromagnastartup.it/en/innovative/startups/smart-city-and-building. [25]

Government of the Netherlands (2019), *Climate Agreement*, https://www.government.nl/documents/reports/2019/06/28/climate-agreement. [8]

IEA (2020), *The Netherlands 2020 Energy Policy Review*, https://iea.blob.core.windows.net/assets/93f03b36-64a9-4366-9d5f-0261d73d68b3/The_Netherlands_2020_Energy_Policy_Review.pdf (accessed on 28 January 2022). [9]

International Carbon Action Partnership (2021), *German National Emissions Trading System*, https://icapcarbonaction.com/en/?option=com_etsmap&task=export&format=pdf&layout=list&systems[]=108#:~:text=Germany%20launched%20its%20National%20Emissions,and%20transport%20fuels%20in%202021.&text=The%20national%20ETS%20will%20be,maximum%20prices%20will%. [4]

Knauf Insulation (2021), *Insulation Matters Annual Review 2021*, https://info.knaufinsulation-ts.com/hubfs/Knauf%20Insulation_%20Insulation%20Matters%20Annual%20Review%202021.pdf?utm_campaign=2021%20-%20Sustainability%20report%20-%20FR&utm_medium=email&_hsmi=130114642&_hsenc=p2ANqtz-_tuwubcXWxP0tXnILqiFmF09KF83KHkrlQqQ (accessed on 28 January 2022). [17]

Ministry of Economic Affaris and Employment of Finland (n.d.), *Network-based Competence Centre for Sustainable and Innovative Public Procurement (KEINO)*, https://tem.fi/en/keino-en. [12]

Ministry of the Ecological Transition (2021), *RE2020: Éco-construire pour le comfort de tous*, https://www.ecologie.gouv.fr/sites/default/files/2021.02.18_DP_RE2020_EcoConstruire_0.pdf (accessed on 29 January 2022). [2]

MLIT (2021), "The committee on energy efficiency measures for houses and buildings for a zero-carbon society", Japanese Ministry of Land, Infrastructure, Transport and Tourism, https://www.mlit.go.jp/jutakukentiku/house/jutakukentiku_house_tk4_000188.html (accessed on 16 January, 2022). [1]

MLIT (2019), "The study on the impacts of energy efficiency renovations on the physical health of residents", Japanese Ministry of Land, Infrastructure, Transport and Tourism, https://www.mlit.go.jp/common/001270049.pdf (accessed on 30 November 2020). [7]

Natural Resources Canada (2022), *Government of Canada*, https://www.canada.ca/en/natural-resources-canada/news/2022/01/minister-wilkinson-provides-update-to-canada-greener-homes-initiative-including-more-energy-advisors-coming-to-manitoba.html (accessed on 10 March 2022). [14]

Natural Resources Canada (2020), *Government of Canada Invests in Energy Efficiency Training for Canadians*, https://www.canada.ca/en/natural-resources-canada/news/2020/07/government-of-canada-invests-in-energy-efficiency-training-for-canadians.html. [13]

OECD (2021), "No net zero without SMEs: Exploring the key issues for greening SMEs and green entrepreneurship", *OECD SME and Entrepreneurship Papers*, No. 30, OECD Publishing, Paris, https://dx.doi.org/10.1787/bab63915-en. [10]

OECD (2020), "Cities policy responses", *OECD Policy Responses to Coronavirus (COVID-19)*, OECD, Paris, https://www.oecd.org/coronavirus/policy-responses/cities-policy-responses-fd1053ff/ (accessed on 24 October, 2021). [18]

PAW (n.d.), *Factsheet: Programme for Natural Gas-free Districts*. [21]

SFWPS (n.d.), *Municipal Buildings Energy Benchmarking*, San Francisco Water Power Sewer, https://sfpuc.org/about-us/reports/municipal-buildings-energy-benchmarking#:~:text=Power%20BI%20Report&text=In%202011%2C%20the%20San%20Francisco,and%20disclose%20building%20energy%20performance. (accessed on 25 January 2022). [16]

U.S. Department of Energy (n.d.), *Better Buildings Financing Navigator*, https://betterbuildingssolutioncenter.energy.gov/financing-navigator/option/green-bonds. [20]

Annex A. Questionnaire of OECD Survey on Decarbonising Buildings in Cities and Regions

Subnational policies and challenges

Section 1. Subnational plans and strategies

1.1. Does your region/city have dedicated plans or strategies on energy efficiency in buildings?

- Energy efficiency in buildings as stand-alone plans or strategies
    - Yes
    - Ongoing, in development
    - No
- Energy efficiency in buildings as part of broader regional/municipal energy plans or strategies
    - Yes
    - Ongoing, in development
    - No
- Energy efficiency in buildings as part of broader regional/municipal climate plans or strategies
    - Yes
    - Ongoing, in development
    - No
- Energy efficiency in buildings as part of COVID-19 recovery plans or strategies
    - Yes
    - Ongoing, in development
    - No

    If you answered "yes" to one of above choices, please provide the names of plans or strategies and the links to websites and documents, if available.

1.1.1. If you answered "Yes" to the previous question, do they have quantitative targets and monitoring indicators related to energy efficiency in the building?

- Yes, they have both quantitative targets and monitoring indicators.
- Yes, they only have quantitative targets.
- No, they do not have quantitative targets nor monitoring indicators.
- Other. Please specify: _____.

If you answered "Yes" or "Other", please provide a description on specific policy targets/goals for improving energy efficiency in the building sector and whether your policies/strategies prioritise certain types of buildings (e.g. single-family homes, condominiums, social housing, office buildings, public buildings, etc.).

1.1.2. If you answered "Yes" to the previous question, are these targets incorporated in the municipal/regional investment planning process to support the identification/prioritisation of the municipal/regional investments?

- o Yes
- o No

If you answered "Yes", please provide a description on what systems are in place to monitor progress in achieving these targets (e.g. monitoring how the annual investment plan is contributing to these targets).

1.2. What are the <u>three key priorities</u> in promoting energy efficiency in buildings for your city or region?

- Please select **three key priorities only** that need to be done to advance energy efficiency in buildings, including "Other".
    - o New or updated subnational plan or strategy on buildings
    - o Stricter building energy codes / minimum legal requirement
    - o Greater use of public building procurement
    - o Greater support to innovative local projects and initiatives
    - o Greater capacity building effort in subnational governments
    - o Broader engagement of citizens and the private sector / greater awareness raising
    - o Greater support to technology development
    - o New or enhanced database on energy efficiency in buildings
    - o Active co-operation to national policy implementation
    - o Other

    If you chose "Other", please specify.

1.3. In your city/region, how would you assess the primary benefits of energy efficiency in buildings?

- Please assess each of the benefits by their level of importance in the view of your region/city. For instance, your region/city may consider all the benefits to be "very important" or only one of the benefits to be "very important" – please tick the boxes accordingly.

	Very important	Moderately important	Not important
Reduction of greenhouse gas emissions			
Decreased air pollution			
Job creation and economic competitiveness in green industries			
Reduction of energy consumption and increased energy independence			
More comfortable and productive working spaces			
More comfortable homes			
Reduced cost of paying the energy bill for low-income households			
Other			

If you chose "Other", please specify.

Section 2. Local specificities

2. What are the major local specificities and/or unique contexts related to energy efficiency in buildings? Does your region/city recognise them as strengths/opportunities or weakness/threats?

Local specificities/Unique contexts	Strength/Opportunity	Weakness/Threat	N/A
Climate (heating/cooling degree days)			
Volume of old building stock			
Volume of social housing stock			
House price and housing affordability			
Energy price and energy affordability			
Volume of new construction/renovation			
Location of universities and research institutes			
Preparedness/skill of local construction firms			
Administrative capacity of local authorities			
Financing for energy efficiency retrofits			
Other			

If you chose "Other", please specify.

Optional: Please provide a brief development on your above choices.

Section 3. Subnational policy measures

1) Building energy codes

3.1. Are building energy codes in place in your region/city?

- o Yes, mandatory building energy codes in place
- o Yes, voluntary building energy codes in place
- o No, but codes in development
- o No, no building energy codes in place

3.1.1. If you answered "Yes" to the previous question, to what types of buildings are the building energy codes applied in your region/city?

- Please tick all applicable boxes.
  - o Only new buildings
  - o Existing buildings when conducting a certain scale of renovation, in addition to new buildings
  - o Existing buildings when rented or sold, in addition to new buildings
  - o All existing buildings
  - o Other

If you chose "Other", please specify.

3.1.2. If you answered "Yes" to Question 3.1, does your region/city have its own regional/local building energy codes?

- o Yes, its own regional/local building energy codes
- o No, utilising national building energy codes (or equivalent)

3.1.3. If you answered "Yes" to the previous question, do the regional/local building energy codes require a higher level of energy efficiency than the national building energy codes?

- o Yes, a much higher level
- o Yes, a slightly higher level
- o No, the same or lower level
- o Unable to compare the levels

3.1.4. If you answered "Yes" to Question 3.1.2, does the regional/local building energy codes require the level of net-zero energy buildings (or equivalent)?

- o Yes, for part of new buildings
- o Yes, for all new buildings
- o Yes, for part of existing buildings in addition to new buildings
- o Yes, for other sets of buildings
- o No

If you chose "Yes, for part of new buildings", "Yes, for part of existing buildings" or "Yes, for other sets of buildings", please specify the types of buildings.

3.2. What other regional/local regulatory measures does your region/city take, related to energy efficiency in buildings?

- Please tick all applicable boxes.
  - o Zoning regulations (e.g. energy efficient building zones)
  - o Energy efficiency requirements for buildings built on lands owned by subnational governments
  - o Mandatory reporting (e.g. energy consumption, carbon emissions)
  - o Mandatory building certification (e.g. green building certifications)
  - o Other

If you chose "Other", please specify.

In the open-response box below, please elaborate on the option(s) you selected.

2) Public buildings

3.3. Does your region/city promote energy efficiency measures for public buildings?

- o Yes
- o No

3.3.1. If you answered "Yes" to the previous question, what types of public buildings are targeted?

- Please tick all applicable boxes.
    - Offices (e.g. subnational government offices)
    - Education (e.g. public schools and universities)
    - Healthcare
    - Medical
    - Public housing
    - Other (e.g. libraries, community centres, sports facilities)

3.3.2. If you answered "Yes" to Question 3.3, what types of energy efficiency measures does your region/city promote for public buildings?

- Please tick all applicable boxes.
    - Energy efficiency renovations/retrofits
    - Construction of energy efficient buildings
    - Energy efficient appliances and equipment
    - Digital technologies (e.g. smart efficient buildings, grid-interactive buildings, smart meters)
    - Renewable energy use (e.g. solar PV, solar heaters)
    - Other

    If you chose "Other", please specify.

    In the open-response box below, please elaborate on the option(s) you selected.

3.3.3. If you answered "Yes" to Question 3.3, does your region/city require higher level of energy efficiency for public buildings than the national building energy codes?

- Yes, a much higher level
- Yes, a slightly higher level
- No, the same or lower level
- Unable to compare the levels
- No specific standard or criteria

3.3.4. If you answered "Yes" to Question 3.3, does your region/city require the level of net-zero energy buildings (or equivalent) for public buildings?

- Yes
- Yes, for part of new buildings
- Yes, for all new buildings
- Yes, for part of existing buildings in addition to new buildings
- Other
- No

If you chose "Yes, for part of new buildings", "Yes, for part of existing buildings" or "Yes, for other sets of buildings", please specify the types of buildings.

3) Financial incentives/financing mechanisms

3.4. Does your region/city provide its own financial incentives or financing mechanisms for energy efficiency measures in buildings?

- o Yes, its own financial incentives or financial mechanisms
- o No, utilising nationally provided financial incentives or financing mechanisms
- o No, no financial incentives or financing mechanisms provided

3.4.1. If you answered "Yes" to the previous question, for what types of energy efficiency measures does your region/city provide financial incentives or financing mechanisms?

- Please tick all applicable boxes.
    - o Energy efficiency renovations/retrofits in general
    - o Energy efficiency renovations/retrofits for low-income households (e.g. energy poor)
    - o Construction of energy efficient buildings
    - o Energy efficient appliances and equipment
    - o District-scale energy management system (e.g. district energy, energy storage facilities, co-generation systems and EV batteries)
    - o Digital technologies (e.g. smart efficient buildings, grid-interactive buildings, smart meters)
    - o Renewable energy use (e.g. solar photovoltaic, solar heaters)
    - o Other

    If you chose "Other", please specify.

3.4.2. If you answered "Yes" to Question 3.4, what types of financial incentives or financial mechanisms does your region/city provide?

- Please tick all applicable boxes.
    - o Support to administrative costs (e.g. monitoring actual energy savings)
    - o Tax exemptions
    - o Grants
    - o Loans and loan guarantees
    - o Auctions and obligations (e.g. obligations imposed on energy retailers or distributors to achieve specific energy efficiency outcomes)
    - o Mortgages (e.g. preferential interest rates for energy efficient homes)
    - o Small scale financing (e.g. on-bill financing, on-tax financing)
    - o Green bonds
    - o Promotion of new business models (e.g. cooling as a service, heating as a service, energy service company, or ESCO)
    - o Other

    If you chose "Other", please specify.

    In the open-response box below, elaborate on the option(s) you selected in Question 3.4.1 and 3.4.2.

4) Other policy measures

3.5. What other types of policy measures does your region/city take to enhance energy efficiency in buildings?

- Please tick all applicable boxes.
    - Citizen engagement (e.g. campaigns, "one-stop shop" technical assistance)
    - Support to local industry (e.g. skill development for small and medium-sized local businesses)
    - Private sector engagement (e.g. platform for local businesses related to energy efficiency in buildings)
    - Capacity building in subnational governments (e.g. code enforcement, public procurement)
    - Pilot and demonstration projects (e.g. low-carbon district developments)
    - Locally tailored analysis and planning (e.g. local database on building energy performance)
    - None
    - Other

    If you chose "Other", please specify.

    In the open-response box below, please elaborate on the option(s) you selected.

Section 4. Obstacles

4.1. What are the three greatest obstacles to enhancing energy efficiency in buildings in your region/city?

- Please select **three key obstacles only**, including "Other".
    - Lack of political momentum
    - Insufficient budget
    - Insufficient human resources and technical expertise
    - Lack of financial incentives for property owners
    - Lack of motivation for property owners (e.g. "split incentives", difficulty of reaching co-investment decision in multifamily residences)
    - Institutional fragmentation across relevant departments and agencies
    - Insufficient local market size to bring in private investment
    - Lack of incentives from national regulations for developing new business models
    - Insufficient speed of industry (e.g. contractors, professionals) in responding to needed innovations and new technologies
    - Insufficient data and analysis on local building stock and policy measures
    - Other

    If you chose "Other", please specify.

    In the open-response box below, please elaborate on the option(s) you selected.

4.2. What are the current data and information gaps that prevent the understanding of where your city and region stand in terms of energy efficiency in buildings?

- Please rate the following statements, according to your level of agreement: "strongly agree" / "agree" / "disagree" / "strongly disagree" / "unsure or no opinion

	Strongly agree	Agree	Disagree	Strongly disagree	Unsure or no opinion
Your city/region has data/information gaps on monitoring current status and outcomes on energy efficiency in buildings (e.g. lack of data on energy consumption from buildings or energy performance of buildings in your city/region)					
Your city/region has data/information gaps on providing a clear rationale for citizens to invest in energy efficiency measures in buildings (e.g. benefits of energy efficiency in buildings for individuals or local communities are unclear)					
Your city/region has data/information gaps on developing a clearly defined local plan or strategy related to energy efficiency in buildings (e.g. a lack of building stock data, unclear which buildings to target)					
Your city/region has data/information gaps on assessing its policies compared to peer city/region (e.g. a lack of comparable data on policy framework condition or energy efficiency outcomes)					

Optional: In the open-response box, please provide any additional information: for instance, information on specific data/information gaps or how your region/city is going to address them. (Where possible, please also outline any ongoing efforts to utilise digital technologies for data collection, analysis and management, e.g. accessing smart meter data, environmental data, advanced analytics, data-driven spatial planning, digital twins, aerial data.)

Section 5. Policy co-ordination and stakeholder engagement

5.1. To which ministry is the local authority with power of mandate on energy efficiency in buildings linked?

- Please tick all applicable boxes.
    - Ministry of Energy (or equivalent)
    - Ministry of Housing and Urban Development (or equivalent)
    - Ministry of Environment (or equivalent)
    - Other

    If you chose "Other", please specify.

5.2. How well are energy efficiency policies in buildings co-ordinated across and between levels of government in your country?

- Please rate the following statements, according to your level of agreement: "strongly agree" / "agree" / "unsure or no opinion / "disagree" / "strongly disagree"

	Strongly agree	Agree	Disagree	Strongly disagree	Unsure or no opinion
There is good horizontal policy co-ordination on energy efficiency in buildings across sectoral agencies/department within your region/city					
There is good horizontal policy co-ordination on energy efficiency in buildings, between your region/city and other regions/cities (e.g. multiple local administrative entities spread across/beyond a large urban area)					
There is good vertical policy co-ordination on energy efficiency in buildings, between your region/city and the national government					

In the open-response box, please provide any additional information: for instance, if you can elaborate on specific vertical and horizontal policy co-ordination challenges and how your region/city/country is addressing them.

5.3. Beyond governments, which types of stakeholders <u>in the private and utilities sectors</u> are engaged in policy making and implementation related to energy efficiency in buildings?

- Please tick all applicable boxes.
    - Construction
    - Architecture
    - Building inspection
    - Real estate
    - Utilities (electricity, gas, etc.)
    - Energy service company (ESCO)
    - Equipment manufacturing (heating, air conditioning, ventilation, lighting, etc.)
    - Financial service
    - Local business in general
    - Other
    - None

    If you chose "Other", please specify.

5.4. Beyond governments, which types of stakeholders <u>in civil society and non-profit organisations</u> are engaged in policy making and implementation related to energy efficiency in buildings?

- Please tick all applicable boxes.
    - Public housing authorities
    - Social housing owners
    - Building/homeowners associations
    - Landlords associations

- Non-profit organisations
- Academia/research institutes/universities
- Citizens
- Other
- None

If you chose "Other", please specify.

5.5. Which mechanisms are used to engage these stakeholders?

- Please tick all applicable boxes.
  - Consultation (meetings, workshops, forums, etc.)
  - Multimedia communication strategy to inform the public and stakeholders on the policy-making process
  - Open access to policy documents and data
  - Co-drafting, partnership (where input has been actively taken into account to shape the policy)
  - Official public hearings and discussions
  - Other
  - None

  If you chose "Other", please specify.

  In the open-response box below, please elaborate on the option(s) you selected in Question 5.3, 5.4 and 5.5.

Section 6. Support from national government and supranational and international donors

6.1. Do you think your region/city has enough support (e.g. financial, technical, human resources) from the national government to enhance energy efficiency in buildings?

- Yes
- No

6.2. Which types of support from the national government does your region/city need further?

- Please tick all applicable boxes.
  - Removing barriers in national regulations that inhibit innovative local actions
  - Technical support for developing local plans, strategies or building energy codes
  - Capacity-building support (e.g. code enforcement, public building procurement)
  - Financial support to advance pilot projects in cities and regions
  - Territorial considerations in national plan, strategy or regulations (e.g. differentiated supports/building codes for different types of cities/regions)
  - Database on energy efficiency in buildings with localised indicators and benchmarks
  - Knowledge sharing of best technologies and practices
  - Platform for public private partnership (e.g. between subnational governments and relevant national private sectors)

- o Awareness raising among general public
- o Other

If you chose "Other", please specify.

In the open-response box below, please elaborate on the option(s) you selected.

6.3. *To what extent does your region/city utilise funding or support from multilateral development banks, supranational or other international donors, with regard to energy efficiency in buildings?*

- Please rate the extent to which your region/city utilise funding/support from the following organisations, according to the level of utilisation: "extensively" / "moderately" / "not at all" and provide corresponding names of organisations.

	Extensively	Moderately	Not at all	
Multilateral development banks				
Supranational organisations (e.g. European Union)				
Other international donors				

In the open-response box below, please provide additional information (e.g. names of organisations, fund/facilities and projects, year, and amount of funding) on your above choices.

Section 7. Challenges and opportunities related to COVID-19 and recovery packages

7.1. *How has the COVID-19 crisis affected your city's or region's actions on energy efficiency improvement in buildings?*

- Please tick all applicable boxes.
  - o Slowdown due to declining construction activity
  - o Less public expenditure for energy efficiency in buildings due to rising public deficit
  - o Greater public expenditure for energy efficiency in buildings from COVID-19 recovery packages
  - o Less demand for private energy efficiency investment in buildings due to economic downturn
  - o Greater demand for home retrofits or renovations (including energy efficiency) as a place to telework
  - o Greater needs for energy efficiency retrofits or renovations for low-income households to ensure energy affordability
  - o Other

If you chose "Other", please specify.

Optional: In the open-response box below, please elaborate on the option(s) you selected.

7.2. Does your region/city think that energy efficiency measures in buildings will contribute to the COVID-19 recovery?

- Yes
- No

7.3. Does the COVID-19 recovery plan/strategy of your region/city include energy efficiency measures in buildings?

- Yes
- No

7.4. If you answered "Yes" to the previous question, which types of energy efficiency measures are they?

- Please tick all applicable boxes.
    - Construction of energy efficient public housing
    - Energy efficient renovations of public housing
    - Provide financial incentives for construction of energy efficient private/social housing
    - Provide financial incentives for energy efficient renovations of private/social housing
    - Promote investment in digitalised energy management
    - Other

    If you chose "Other", please specify.

    In the open-response box below, please elaborate on the option(s) you selected.

Section 8. Other

8. *Optional*: Please provide additional information, if there are any particular examples or more information with regard to building energy efficiency policies that you did not mention in the previous questions.

Data and indicators relating to energy efficiency in buildings (OPTIONAL)

Please provide the available data on the following indicators of your region/city for the year 2010 and 2019 (or the most recent available year before 2019) by filling in the following tables. Please also indicate the data sources and the hyperlinks (if public).

Section 9. Basic data

Demographic and socioeconomic data

Indicator	2010	2019	Data source (hyperlinks or contact details)
Population [persons]			
Population density [persons/km^2]			
GDP per capita [local currency/capita]			
Share of household expenditures on energy (electricity, gas and other housing fuels) [%]			
Excess winter deaths index [%] *(the excess of average daily deaths in winter (December to March) compared with non-winter months from the preceding August to November and the following April to July, expressed as a percentage)*			

Energy consumption and renewable energy

Indicator	2010	2019	Data source (hyperlinks or contact details)
Total energy consumption [PJ]			
Energy consumption in Residential Sector [PJ] *(Residential sector may be described differently depending on the country, for example, "Household sector" or "Housing sector".)*			
Energy consumption in Non-residential Sector [PJ] *(Non-residential sector may be described differently depending on the country, such as "Commercial sector" or "Tertiary sector".)*			
Renewable energy consumption [in petajoules, or PJ] *(Consumption of energy from renewable sources such as hydropower, wind and solar.)*			
Distributed solar PV capacity [GW]			

Section 10. Data on building stock

Residential building stock

Indicator	2019 [# of dwellings]	2019 [m²]	Data source (hyperlinks or contact details)
Total dwellings (stock)			
Dwellings built before 1970			
Single-family dwellings (*dwellings such as detached houses and semi-detached houses*)			
Multifamily dwellings (*dwellings such as apartments, flats and condominiums*)			
Public housing (*rental housing provided by public authorities*)			
Social housing other than public housing (*rental housing provided at sub-market prices, excluding public housing*)			
Dwellings annually constructed			

Non-residential building stock

Indicator	2019 [# of buildings]	2019 [m²]	Data source (hyperlinks or contact details)
Total non-residential buildings (stock)			
Non-residential buildings built before 1970			
Public buildings owned by national government or relevant agencies			
Public buildings owned by regional/local governments or relevant agencies			
Non-residential buildings annually constructed			

Section 11. Data on building energy performance

Residential buildings

Indicator	2010	2019	Data source (hyperlinks or contact details)
Average U-value of residential buildings [W/m2K] (average thermal transmittance of residential buildings, which indicates the level of insulation)			
Share of dwellings compliant with local building energy codes [%]			
Share of dwellings that have taken energy performance certification or other voluntary certifications [%]			
Number of dwellings certified as zero-energy buildings or equivalent [# of dwellings]			
Number of dwellings annually undergoing energy efficient renovations [# of dwellings]			
Residential energy consumption per floor space in single-family dwellings [kWh/m2/year]			
Residential energy consumption per floor space in multifamily dwellings [kWh/m2/year]			

Non-residential buildings

Indicator	2010	2019	Data source (hyperlinks or contact details)
Share of non-residential buildings compliant with local building energy codes [%]			
Share of non-residential buildings that have taken energy performance certification or other voluntary certifications [%]			
Number of non-residential buildings certified as zero-energy buildings or equivalent [# of buildings]			
Number of non-residential buildings annually undergoing energy efficient renovations [# of buildings]			

www.ingramcontent.com/pod-product-compliance
Ingram Content Group UK Ltd.
Pitfield, Milton Keynes, MK11 3LW, UK
UKHW050412240426
12048UKWH00020B/1479